WHY
FAITH

MAKES SENSE

WHY
FAITH

MAKES SENSE

Reasons You Can Believe God Is Real

WILL DAVIS JR.

Revell

a division of Baker Publishing Group
Grand Rapids, Michigan

© 2008 by Will Davis Jr.

Published by Revell
a division of Baker Publishing Group
P.O. Box 6287, Grand Rapids, MI 49516-6287
www.revellbooks.com

Printed in the United States of America

Library of Congress Cataloging-in-Publication Data
Davis, Will, 1962–
    Why faith makes sense : reasons you can believe God is real / Will Davis, Jr.
      p.   cm.
    Includes bibliographical references (p.   ).
    ISBN 978-0-8007-3248-6 (pbk.)
    1. Apologetics. I. Title.
  BT1103.D39 2008
  239—dc22
                                                    2008019659

To my dad, Will D. Davis.
You showed me the mountains,
and the mountains showed me God.
Thank you.

Contents

Author's Preface

Thank you in advance for reading *Why Faith Makes Sense*. I pray it encourages you. Here are a couple things you might want to keep in mind as you read through the text.

First, I have aimed for brevity and simplicity over profundity. In the pages that follow, we're going to look at some lofty concepts. Topics like mystery, revelation, evolution, humanism, wisdom, faith, and some of the most difficult aspects of the Christian message are thoroughly discussed. But they are presented in a way that I hope will speak most clearly to the beginning student of these ideas—whether Christian, spiritual seeker, or skeptic.

Second, I have examined these topics as a follower of Christ. I write as one who finds no contradiction between thinking on a rational level and possessing a believing faith. I have tried to express as simply and objectively as possible the agreement between these two supposedly mutually exclusive concepts. When I examine concepts or ideas that I disagree with or don't believe in, I try to present their basic tenets with accuracy and objectivity, often letting the spokespeople for those concepts speak for themselves.

May God bless you and speak to you as you read. "You will seek me and find me when you seek me with all your heart" (Jer. 29:13).

Will Davis Jr.

Acknowledgments

Thanks to . . .

Susie—for loving me, supporting me, praying for me, and putting up with me.

Will III, Emily, and Sara—for always playing along when I say, "You know that's an accident, don't you?"

Jackie Lebihan—for pushing me over the edge with your original, innocent question. Now you are a wonderful, mature believer. Yea, God!

Dave Panos—for sharing your story. You are a mighty man.

Kathy Burke—for sending me a thought-provoking email and inspiring chapter 9.

The faithful attendees of the Ask Any Question class—for providing a forum for me to hash out some of the concepts in this book.

Dr. Francis Collins—for dialoguing with me about the tensions between faith and science. You are an inspiration to many believers.

John R. W. Stott—for your book *Your Mind Matters*, which first encouraged me to study the relationship between faith and the mind. Thanks for inspiring me.

Rick Reynolds—for pushing me to always be above reproach.

Joni Kendrick—for a decade of great friendship and partnership in ministry.

Tonya Parrott—for your amazing support, hard work, proofing, insights, and comments. You are a pleasure to work with.

Gary Sinclair—for being a fellow mountain lover, and for great friendship, comments, and support on this project.

Wendy Browning—for your continued support of, interest in, and contributions to my writing, and for being a good friend.

Gary Bourque—for helpful comments on the early chapters.

Terri Crow—for being, without exception, the world's greatest proofreader. Thanks for believing in and investing in me.

Curt and Andrea Smith—for being kind friends and kingdom servants. I thank God for you daily.

Les Stobbe—for supporting this book concept and being a great example of a godly man.

Vicki Crumpton—for your expertise and great counsel. You have a gift and are a blast to work with. Thank you for seeing the potential in this manuscript and pushing me to make it better.

Suzie Cross Burden—for your amazing support and belief in my writing. God has greatly used you to encourage me. You are a godly woman.

Karen Steele, Brooke Nolen, Claudia Marsh, Deonne Beron, Cheryl Van Andel, and the awesome team at Revell—for the continued excellence of your work and for your kindness to me.

ACF—for being an others-centered church and believing God for more.

The ACF overseers—for believing in me, encouraging my writing, and leading well.

The ACF staff—for being more than co-workers. You are my friends.

Introduction

Do You Really Believe This Stuff?

It happened again just the other day. I was leading a Bible study for a mixed group of people. By "mixed" I mean that the attendees weren't all Christians. In fact, I marketed the Bible study as being primarily for skeptics and the spiritually curious. It was well attended from the first day, with a good number of believers as well as the spiritually unconvinced showing up regularly. In about the sixth or seventh meeting, a young woman attended for the first time. She was in her late twenties, and though she had been raised in church, she was now married to an agnostic and was genuinely unsure of how to classify herself spiritually. However, she remained curious about the validity of the Christian faith. She was attending the Bible study to, in her words, "see if you really had to stop thinking to be a Christian."

Now, I know that this woman meant nothing offensive by her comment. I know that she was merely reciting what she had no doubt heard countless times from the culture in which she lives—that Christianity is for dummies. I smiled politely at her as she spoke; inside I ached. I can't even begin to count the number of times I've heard that sentiment. Somewhere along the line, Christians have been labeled as gullible, and, more importantly, the Christian faith has been tagged as being for the mentally dull.

Why is that? Why have Christians been labeled as non-thinkers? Has the message of Christ really been proven to be the stuff of fairy tales? Has science really invalidated the need for faith? Are Christians really naive, intellectually stunted, and misled?

I'm a Christian. I have made a rational, volitional, and spiritual decision to follow Jesus Christ. I have investigated the claims about his deity, miraculous powers, and resurrection from the dead. I believe them. I find them reasonable and tenable in light of the evidence. I'm a Christian, and I don't think I'm stupid. Sometimes I do and say stupid things, and occasionally I make foolish choices. I may not be the sharpest tool in the shed, but neither am I the dullest.

I wasn't asked to disengage my brain at my baptism. I've never signed any papers requiring me to simply take the Bible at face value and not ask any hard questions. I've never been told that good thinking would get in the way of my beliefs and that I just need to listen to my heart. In fact, my experience has been just the opposite. I've been encouraged to read books and to stretch my mind. I've been challenged to critically scrutinize my belief system and to know not just *what* I believe but *why* I believe it. I've had to wrestle with hard questions to which there seemed to be no satisfactory answers. I've repeatedly had to examine my faith, which is constantly being called into question by science and higher learning. I bet you have too.

If you are a Christ-follower, or if you have given serious thought to becoming one, then you have encountered the cultural skepticism toward the Christian faith. You've probably read the headlines, seen the documentaries, and studied the textbooks that declare that matters of faith are best left in the camp of Santa and the tooth fairy. Whether it's the powerful media mogul who says Christians are all sadly mistaken, the famous film director who produces documentaries challenging the Christian faith, or the scientist-turned-writer who says science has proven that there is no God, the antagonists to the Christian faith, while comparatively few in number, are quite vocal.

You may have felt the sting when some world-renowned thinker called into question the mental capacity of anyone who believes in the divine. For instance, bestselling American atheist Sam Harris, in his book *Letter to a Christian Nation*, said that the fact that nearly half of American adults not only believed in but would welcome the immediate return of Christ was a "moral and intellectual emergency."[1] His book was his "response" to this emergency and his effort to lead poor and confused believers to higher intellectual ground. World-renowned British zoologist and outspoken atheist Richard Dawkins could hardly suppress his disdain for Christians when he commented, "It is completely as I would expect that American scientists are less religious than the American public generally, and that the most distinguished scientists are the least religious of all. What is remarkable is the polar opposition between the religiosity of the American public at large and the atheism of the intellectual elite."[2]

Such derogatory comments toward believers, including believing scientists, are becoming more common and are growing increasingly hostile. How should believers and spiritually inquisitive adults respond? Has science really invalidated faith?

Let me put my cards on the table. Your faith isn't foolish, and there's no need for you to get flustered or feel intimidated when someone says otherwise. It is neither intellectually irresponsible nor illogical to believe in what can't be seen. The very fact that a person considers the claims of Christ and subsequently embraces them is evidence of a mind at work, not at rest. Becoming a Christ-follower does not mean taking a mental sabbatical, and you're not asked to believe *in spite of* what your brain tells you. In fact, Christianity requires people to think more as their faith becomes more profound. Despite reports to the contrary, thinking and believing are not mutually exclusive.

In the pages that follow, you will learn that the Bible is not only reliable as the source document for Christianity, but it is also a book for thinking people. You will see that God expects those who believe in him to bolster their beliefs with their minds. You'll learn that faith is nothing more than reason and intellect at their highest levels.

By the time you're finished with this book, you'll have a much better understanding of the role the mind plays in authentic Christian faith. You'll have more insight into concepts such as ultimate mystery, revelation, and God's communication with human beings. You will learn about major problems with Darwin's theory of evolution and how it can't prove that God doesn't exist. Finally, you'll know why Jesus Christ is God's answer to our ultimate search for wisdom and knowledge.

Why Faith Makes Sense

Intrigued? If you consider yourself a thinker but are unsure of how faith and reason fit together, or if you're a Christian who has never really made the connection between your heart and your head, then I invite you to keep reading. The Bible says we are to love God with all our hearts, souls, and *minds* (see Matt. 22:37; Mark 12:30). Do you want to know just how critical the mind is in matters of faith? If so, then stay tuned, and be sure to put on your thinking cap. Actually, if you're pursuing matters of faith, you already have.

THE GOD CODE

I had started this journey of intellectual exploration to con-
firm my atheism. That now lay in ruins as the argument from
the Moral Law (and many other issues) forced me to admit
the plausibility of the God hypothesis. Agnosticism, which
had seemed like a safe second-place haven, now loomed like
the great cop-out that it often is. Faith in God now seemed
more rational than disbelief.

Dr. Francis Collins,
director of the Human Genome Project

1

Everyone Loves a Good Mystery

It was the Wednesday before Easter my freshman year in college, and I was driving from Baylor University in Waco back to my home in Austin for Easter break. I was traveling south on I-35 at about 11 p.m. As I crested a small hill just north of the town of Jarrell, an eighteen-wheeler caught my eye as it veered suddenly to the right and then stopped. Then I saw why. Lying on the white stripe in the middle of the road was the body of a man. About twenty-five yards past him, lying on its side in the median, was a Volkswagen Beetle. The man had apparently lost control of his car, which must have rolled over several times before ejecting him. Debris and the contents of the car were scattered all over the road. It was one of the scariest things I'd ever seen in my life.

The truck driver and I, having both pulled over, ran to the man and reached him at about the same time. Neither of us got too close. We could tell he was badly hurt, and we were afraid to move him. We then realized we had a problem. The man was lying in the center of the southbound lane of I-35, and cars and trucks were whizzing over the crest of the hill, bearing down on the three of us. Neither of us was willing to abandon the poor man, so we instinctively ran up the road a few yards and stood in the way of the oncoming cars. We waved our arms, trying to signal the fast-approaching vehicles. Then we would jump out of the way and watch desperately as the cars began to swerve in an effort to miss us and the man lying just beyond us. I watched in horror as more than a few cars and trucks missed the man's head by mere inches.

I don't know how long that chaos lasted. It seemed like hours, though I'm sure it was only a few minutes. Finally, another trucker stopped and set up some flares. Traffic began to slow down. An off-duty paramedic showed up and frantically attended to the man. And then—now get this, because it's very important—several state troopers showed up and took charge of the scene. An ambulance arrived. The man was still alive, and the troopers said that he would be taken to an Austin hospital. When I was no longer needed at the scene, I walked back to my car and began the rest of my drive home. I was one shaken college freshman.

I spent the next week trying to find out what happened to the man. If he was alive, I intended to visit him in the hospital. I wanted to get to know the guy, pray for him, and encourage him. I never got the chance.

According to the Texas Department of Public Safety, the wreck never happened. I called them on several occasions and gave them the exact location and time of the wreck. I told them how many state troopers were there on the scene. They had absolutely no record of any accidents on that stretch of I-35 in that time frame. No troopers had been dispatched during the time when I had seen and talked to them. No hospitals in the region had received any accident victims by ambulance during that time. I called every hospital in the area, even those well beyond the immediate area; none had admitted my wreck victim. There were no articles in the paper about the accident. It wasn't just that nobody could find him; it was more as if the wreck had never happened.

What did happen? What had I seen, and why was it not recorded anywhere? Did I stumble onto some CIA chase event that quickly became a non-event? Was it a government cover-up? Or was this just another example of really poor record keeping? I'll never know. The incident remains one of the great mysteries of my life.

Do you have some mysteries in your life that remain unsolved? Do you have lingering questions that will bug you until you find out the answers? You probably do. Do you know what is the greatest, most intriguing mystery facing humans today, and one that every human in history has wrestled with? In a word, *God*.

Mystery and Religion

If you highlight the word *mystery* and then push "Shift F7" on your computer keyboard, you'll find synonyms or phrases like *secret, something hidden, problem, enigma, puzzle, riddle,* and *conundrum*. The scholars in Webster world call *mystery* "something not understood or that is beyond understanding; a private secret."[1]

In short, a mystery is something we'd like to know but can't. It's an equation whose solution eludes us, and that makes it all the more alluring. *Mystery* implies that the answer we seek lies somewhere outside of our reach and that we will be unable to secure it without some type of external intervention. Mysteries require clues, hints, or disclosures that help us discover where the truth we seek ultimately lies.

You might be interested to know that Webster's definition for *mystery* I cited above was not the primary one but the secondary one. Webster's primary definition for *mystery* had an unexpected twist to it: "a religious truth that man can know by revelation alone and cannot fully understand."[2]

Did the Webster folks try to pass off *mystery* as something religious? Did they really connect *spiritual revelation* with *mystery*? Maybe my 1977 *Webster's New Collegiate Dictionary* was just a little outdated. So I consulted a much more current (and, might I add, *cooler*) source, the Internet. I Googled Webster's online dictionary and typed in *mystery*. Uh-oh. Now this was getting weird. There was almost the exact same primary definition from the last century: "a religious truth that one can know only by revelation and cannot fully understand."[3] What happened to progress? What about cultural evolution? Where are all the thinkers? Is this a fundamentalist conspiracy or what? What in the world does *mystery* have to do with religion? And the next obvious question is more important: what in the world does *mystery* have to do with God?

Actually, everything. As I stated earlier, there is no greater question humans face than that of the nature of God. He is the ultimate mystery. Does he exist? Is he real? Can he be known? Where did he come from? If humans are accidental and random, why do we spend so much time seeking the divine? Why have philosophers, theologians, thinkers, and poets in every century sought to answer the question of God's existence?

I bet you have as well. I've certainly spent plenty of nights staring into a star-filled sky, wondering about God. I have plenty of questions: If God is real, why does he sometimes seem so silent? Why does he put up with all the junk in the world, especially all the junk that's been done in his name? Why do children suffer and die from starvation when there's more than enough food to feed them in storehouses all around the world? Why doesn't he do something?

If you have ever found yourself wondering why God acts the way he does, you're in good company. King David, the author of most of the book of Psalms, had his own questions: "Why, O LORD, do you stand far off? Why do you hide yourself in times of trouble?" (Ps. 10:1).

Could the dictionary be right? Maybe the answers to these questions about God aren't something we'll ever discover on our own. Maybe we need the intervention or aid of an outside source. Perhaps we need help from a third party so we might ultimately come to the right conclusions.

The Biblical Mystery

Did you know that the Bible talks at length about the mystery of God? In fact, the biblical writer Paul was quite fond of the term. Paul believed that God is an unsolvable mystery. He is simply too grand and otherworldly for us to ever fully know him on our own. The prophet Isaiah, who lived seven hundred years before Paul, put it this way: " 'For my thoughts are not your thoughts, neither are your ways my ways,' declares the LORD. 'As the heavens are higher than the earth, so are my ways higher than your ways and my thoughts than your thoughts' " (Isa. 55:8–9). What Isaiah described in those verses is what Paul often called the *mystery* of God.[4]

The word for *mystery* that Paul used so frequently in his writings is actually a compound word that literally means "to shut the mouth" or "to be silent." The word implies that

25

a mystery is created when the keeper or owner of the mystery's solutions remains silent. This isn't a "no one knows for sure" kind of mystery; it's a "someone knows but isn't telling" kind of mystery. The information required to solve the mystery exists, but its source—whoever holds its secrets and answers—simply hasn't chosen to share it. As long as the source of the answers remains silent, the mystery continues.

In the case of God, he is both the mystery *and* the explanation. He is at the same time the enigma and the code cracker. God is not only what is being sought after (the ultimate mystery), but he is also the only one who can make the answers to the mystery known (through self-disclosure). In the mystery of spiritual realities, God is both source and solution. He is hidden, and he must choose to be found. And that, according to Paul, is exactly what God did. He pulled back the curtain, removed the cloud, blew away the fog, and made himself fully knowable and available by revealing himself. God, the keeper of the ultimate secrets and mysteries of life, has chosen to make the answers known.

To the sophisticates of the ancient Greek city of Ephesus, Paul wrote that the mystery of God had been made known to the world through his divine revelation. To the Christians in Rome, Paul wrote that the mystery of God had been revealed in very clear and specific terms. He declared that the message of God was a "secret which has been kept through times eternal" (see Rom. 16:25–26, from *The Bible in Basic English*) but had now been made undeniably clear by God. Paul encouraged the Roman believers to stay true to their faith, because the message they believed was no myth or legend, but rather the reality of God finally made known. It was reasonable, logical, and believable.

Why Faith Makes Sense

Over six centuries before the time of Christ, the prophet Jeremiah offered a sweeping promise to the nation of Israel: "Call to me and I will answer you and tell you great and unsearchable things you do not know" (Jer. 33:3). Jeremiah promised that God had "great and unsearchable things"—eternal truths, ultimate realities, and the answers to life's most pressing and profound questions—ready to share with us. His implication, however, was that such great truths cannot be discerned without God's help.

So when God chooses to remove the mystery of his existence, when he wants to make himself known, when he decides to pull back the veil and answer the questions about himself, to whom or to what does he speak? In short, your mind. The primary target of God's self-revelation to humans and the main tool you have for receiving and processing God's communication with you is your brain. As we will see in the coming chapters, belief in God doesn't require you to check your brains at the door. In fact, the process of belief begins with your mind.

2

Contact

It was called the Sea of Tranquility, and it was chosen for its gentle landscape. Located precisely at 00.67408° N latitude and 23.47297° E longitude, *Mare Tranquillitatis* seemed like the perfect landing site for humanity's first romp on the moon. But even with its relatively smooth terrain, Commander Neil Armstrong had to make a last-minute adjustment to avoid landing the *Eagle* in the midst of a 180-meter-wide and 30-meter-deep crater. The *Eagle*, the landing module of NASA's Apollo 11 mission, set down peacefully about six kilometers from its original landing site at 4:17 p.m. EDT on July 20, 1969. Just over six hours later, Commander Armstrong made his now-famous "one small step for man" onto the moon, and for the first time in history, humans were walking on the surface of our nearest celestial neighbor.

Tranquility Base, the nickname Armstrong gave the *Eagle*'s landing area, proved to be a safe haven for the astronauts. Only a few days after setting down, the *Eagle* uneventfully

left the moon to reunite with the command module or-
biting above and eventually returned safely to Earth. The
first moon outing had been a great success and without
incident. We had walked on the moon's surface and lived
to tell about it.

It may seem obvious, but I'd like to point out that the
choice of Tranquility Base was not random. NASA scientists
did not spin a globe of the moon, stick a pin on a point, and
say, "I think we'll land . . . here." They actually spent years
in research, planning, and study to determine the best possible sites and backup sites for the Apollo missions. Every
detail had to be thought out, every contingency considered.
No mission of such importance, of such expense, and with
so much potential danger could ever be approached haphazardly. NASA harnessed some of the greatest engineers,
mathematicians, and scientists in the world to make sure
that Apollo 11 and her precious cargo were set up to win.
Tranquility Base was established only because NASA of-
ficials selected, prepared for, and targeted the exact place
where they intended to first land on the moon.

So what happened when God wanted to first communicate with humans? Did he select, prepare for, and target
the details of how, when, and where he would first connect
with his creation? Did he have a strategic plan, or was it
random? Is there any rhyme or reason to God's attempts to
make himself known to us, or are they haphazard? Surely a
mission of such critical importance required forethought
and planning. Did God just spin the likeness of a human,
touch it at some random point, and say, "I think I'll land
. . . here," or was it strategic? Is there a preferred landing
zone of spiritual first contact? Has God determined a point
where we are to meet him, and if so, how do we know
where it is?

Let's consider the human mind. It's hidden safely in the perfectly formed protective cavity between your ears. In fact, you're using part of it to process the letters, words, thoughts, and ideas that you are reading right now. Tranquility Base is in your mind, and it's there that God initially reveals to you the mystery of his nature.

Allow Me to Introduce . . . God

God, by definition, is infinite. Try as we may to know him, God, by his very nature, eludes our grasp. If God could be proven by a hypothesis, reproduced in a laboratory, or measured and quantified in some way, then he would not be God. Thus, the only way God can be known is if and when he chooses to be. If we are to find God, then he must lead us to himself. And when God leads us to discover him, he uses *revelation*.[1]

Revelation is the disclosure of information that cannot be discovered and is not readily accessible. In biblical thinking, *revelation* is the solution side of *mystery*. If *mystery* is something that cannot be discovered—something hidden from our knowledge—then *revelation* is what happens when the keeper of the secrets chooses to make the information known. Mysteries are solved through *revelation*.

Revelation happens when a wife tells her husband that she is expecting a baby. It's *revelation* when a criminal discloses the details of an unsolved crime. We call it *revelation* when a government agency or the White House releases information that we would otherwise have never had access to. You hear those statements frequently in the media: "The White House revealed today . . ." "Startling new revelations in the trial of . . ." You get the picture. *Revelation* is receiving information from a third party that you otherwise wouldn't know.

Take, for example, an experience I once had while buying sunglasses. I was at a sporting goods store looking at a couple pairs of my favorite outdoor glasses—Oakleys. Oakleys are cool, Oakleys are hip, Oakleys are durable, and Oakleys are great for outdoor eye protection.

I was looking at myself in the mirror at the glasses display, trying to determine which pair of Oakleys would best fit my rugged, outdoor lifestyle, when the girl behind the counter asked if I needed some help. She was a twentysomething and seemed sincere in her offer, so I asked, "Which pair looks best on me?" It seemed like a fair question at the time. She stepped back from the counter and took a long look at me. She asked me to try on each pair for her a couple times. I thought, *This girl must really be a pro. She knows exactly what to look for.* Then she spoke: "Well, if you want to know the truth . . . well, let me look at them again. Okay, if you want to know the truth, I mean, both look really good. Okay, but, well, this pair [she referenced the pair I was leaning toward buying], they kind of look like you're trying to be sexy . . . and you're not." That's *revelation.*

Why God Won't Go Away

God never does anything randomly. Despite conventional wisdom that says otherwise, things of value rarely come about haphazardly. Eternal things never do. When God speaks, acts, works, creates, and reveals, it's always deliberate. There is no spiritual Russian roulette with God. He never loads an eternal truth in a chamber, spins the cylinder, and then tries to get lucky. That's simply not how he works. When God launches an eternal truth toward humans, he does so with a specific target in mind. Jesus wasn't born into first-century Palestine by accident. The time, place, and setting of his arrival were very precise. Paul called the event of Jesus's birth "the fullness of the time" (Gal. 4:4 NASB). God knew what he was doing; he had a plan. So it is with God's revelation. He always has a desired outcome, and he always has an intended target. And you can be sure that the target is going to be required to use his or her mind to decipher God's messages. For God, the mind is the port of entry to the human soul. When he establishes contact, he uses thoughts, words, concepts, and ideas.

Did you know that there is an entire field of science dedicated to the connection between our brains and religion? Neurologists and psychologists have coined the term *neurotheology* to describe their study of the role of the mind in humans' religious tendencies. It appears that our brains are wired for religious thought. We seem to be preprogrammed to be spiritual.[2]

That's an interesting concept, isn't it? If humans evolved, how did we ever come to have religious tendencies? And how did our brains actually develop circuits that appear specifically suited for religious thought? Why would we have brain circuitry for religious expression if no outside source to stimulate such brain development exists? In other words, why would we be spiritually minded if there was nothing spiritual wooing us?

Snapshots of Revelation

The Bible is the written record of God's revelation to human minds. The biblical writers, under the guidance and oversight of God's Holy Spirit, did their best to accurately record how, when, and where God made himself known to us. One of the first recorded disclosures of God in the Bible is found in its first book, Genesis. In chapter 28, we find

Jacob, the grandson of the patriarch Abraham, on the run from his brother because he deceived him and stole their father's blessing. After stopping to rest for the night, Jacob had a dream in which he saw God, who promised to give Jacob's descendants the very land on which he was lying. He promised to bless Jacob even though he didn't deserve it. When Jacob awoke, he built a stone monument and named the place *Bethel*, which means "house of God."

How did God speak to Jacob? In a dream. He used Jacob's subconscious mind as the point of initial contact. He chose to communicate with Jacob in such a way that Jacob would hear him loud and clear. When Jacob woke up, he used his memory to recall what God had said, and he used his intellect to interpret the meaning. He then discerned that he had been visited by God. God had revealed himself to a man, given him a promise, and left an impression that he would never forget—and the entire process had taken place in his mind.

Consider some other examples. God revealed to Noah that he was going to destroy humankind by a massive flood. He told Noah to build a huge boat—an ark—and he gave specific dimensions and instructions on how it was to be constructed. We don't know exactly how God spoke to Noah, but we know that Noah processed God's instructions with his mind. When God revealed himself to Abraham and promised that he would become the father of a great nation (Israel), he did so in a vision that Abraham saw in his mind. God appeared to Moses and ordered him to return to Egypt to lead the Israelites out of captivity. He revealed himself through a mysteriously burning desert bush, and he spoke with words Moses could clearly understand. Moses processed his encounter with God and deciphered God's instructions with his mind. The result was that he dropped everything he was doing, went to Egypt, and spent the next forty years leading the people of Israel.

God's Top Ten

Speaking of Moses, have you ever thought about the Ten Commandments? How do you think Moses got them? And what about all the incredible concepts of the Mosaic law, the system of ethics and morals that became the Judeo-Christian standard worldwide—where did they originate? Did Moses just think them up all by himself?

While driving to work recently, I was listening to a popular local call-in radio show. The question *de jure* was the public display of the Ten Commandments in state and federal areas: Is it a violation of the separation of church and state? Should the state advertise such religiously oriented teachings? Well, an amazing thing happened. An atheist called in to offer support for displaying the Ten Commandments. Imagine that! Her logic was simple: the Ten Commandments don't belong just to Christians; they are also recognized by Jews and Muslims. She argued that the Ten Commandments form the basic system of values by which the world has been governed for over three millennia. They are universal and timeless and need to be seen as more than just a religious icon. Talk about an unlikely proponent! The talk-show hosts were speechless.

There's one thing the atheist didn't consider when making her statement: Moses claimed to get the Ten Commandments from God. He came down from the mountain after one of his forty-day retreats and basically said, "Hey, you rebellious people! Look what God gave me!" What God had given him were the ten nonnegotiables by which they were to live in relation to God and each other. Through his miraculous interaction with a human, God gave the world the basic system by which we determine good and bad behavior and govern our societies.

God Calling

In 1 Samuel, the young boy Samuel was brought by his mother to live with Eli the priest in the tabernacle. But even though the boy spent day and night in the most holy and religious place available to a young Hebrew, knowledge of God was not guaranteed for him. The writer recorded that "Samuel did not yet know the LORD: The word of the LORD had not yet been revealed to him" (1 Sam. 3:7). Later on, God spoke to Samuel in very clear words that he could hear. So clearly, in fact, that Samuel at first thought it was Eli calling to him. God was ready to introduce himself to Samuel, and he did it in a way that Samuel could clearly understand.

That experience—God revealing himself to the mind of a human—is actually quite normal. God has been awakening the minds of spiritual seekers to his reality since he first made and interacted with Adam and Eve. God revealed himself to Enoch, and the two walked together throughout Enoch's life. God revealed himself to Abraham in the land of Ur. Have you ever thought about Moses's wise and godly father-in-law, Jethro? He was a priest of Midian. What were the Midianites doing worshiping the God of Israel? It appears that God had revealed himself to them as well.

The Bible has been teaching for centuries that the mind is the primary landing area for initial God-thoughts. The idea of God, according to the Bible, is not the stuff of myth or legend. He is not a figment of our imaginations, and he is not a product of our environment. Rather, the concept of God is viable because his existence is reasonable. People believe in God all over the world today because, in their minds, that makes sense.

The Aftershocks of Revelation

Without revelation, we can never know God. Without revelation, there is no Christianity, because there is nothing in which Christians can believe. And therefore, without revelation, the only god we know is the one we create. But when God connects with a receptive human at the Tranquility Base of the brain, when divine contact is made in the fertile soil of an open and thinking mind, then revelation occurs. God introduces himself.

The theological reality of God's revelation to humans has several implications for all people. *Revelation* is one of the more radical concepts in the Bible, and its impact on how we live and think is far-reaching. In the book of Proverbs, the thinker and philosopher Solomon recorded an interesting insight: "Where there is no revelation, the people cast off restraint; but blessed is he who keeps the law" (Prov. 29:18). The King James Version says it perhaps more poetically: "Where there is no vision, the people perish." In either translation, Solomon's point is humbling. A culture with no sense of overall accountability to a higher source will eventually self-destruct. Without revelation, without a vision for life that comes from a source beyond ourselves, we will indeed be left to our own moral devices. And that, as history has repeatedly proven, is never a good option.

A culture's awareness of revelation creates the tension necessary for that culture to stay on the right track. But when a people group rejects the concept of revelation, when it renders the verdict that there is no upward call of accountability, then it has started down the disastrously slippery slope of casting off restraint. Solomon's words could not be more prophetic and accurate: without a sense of revelation, a nation will eventually die. Like a spacewalking astronaut without a tether or any motorized power pack, we will inevitably drift off into the outer space of moral relativity.

Three broad implications of revelation make it necessary for cultural survival. First, *a people who embrace the reality of revelation must also then embrace the reality of a revealer*. Revelation is never random; it isn't accidental. It always requires an initial message sender. It implies that someone with formerly hidden secrets has acted or spoken so that those secrets can be known. Acknowledging that a truth has been revealed leads to the logical conclusion that someone has done the revealing. Wherever the curtain has been drawn back on an eternal reality, you can be sure that someone has not only created the revealed reality but has also removed the curtain so that it might be known. Cultures and peoples that believe in revelation are more likely to survive because they are, at least to some degree, responding to the ultimate revealer.

Second, *revelation is critical for cultural survival because it implies that there is ultimate accountability*. God never goes to the trouble of revealing himself for his own sake. He doesn't need to. He doesn't need us. God doesn't have to receive our worship or belief to exist. He is entirely self-sustaining. So when he reveals some aspect of himself to a person's mind, it's because he has something that person desperately needs. He's making it known for their sake, not his. And whenever God speaks an eternal truth, a life principle, a moral conviction, or a specific set of instructions into the heart and mind of a person, the message always includes the expectation that the person will respond appropriately. He speaks what we (and probably others) need, and he fully expects us to act on what we have heard and received from him.

Consider Solomon's words: "Where there is no revelation, the people cast off restraint." In other words, without the upward pull of accountability to an ultimate revealer, people have no real reason to behave themselves. Without the sense that one day we will indeed answer for the knowledge of God that we have, we have little motivation to stay on the high road. The gravitational pull of sin and self-gratification are just too strong. But with the reality of revelation, with the personal conviction that there is a moral code and a moral code maker to whom we will answer, we suddenly develop that little check in our spirit, that moral conscience telling us to steer clear of evil, for not only is evil wrong, but we will answer for it.

When it comes to eternal truth, there is no such thing as peer-to-peer revelation. You telling a friend about God is not the same as God telling you about himself. When you speak to a friend about your faith, you're telling what you've learned from someone else, or perhaps from God's Word and the Holy Spirit. You're telling the friend what you ultimately received through God's act of revealing. You're communicating God's truth to an equal. But when God speaks to us directly—when he uses a sunset, a sermon, or a verse of Scripture to pull our hearts toward him—that's not peer-to-peer communication. That's divine-to-human, infinite-to-finite, holy-to-unholy communication. And whenever God speaks to us in our minds, whenever he breaks his silence and shows us truths that we could not have discovered otherwise, whenever he chooses to make himself known, it always includes accountability.

Finally, *revelation implies that humans are preprogrammed to receive messages from God.* As I'm writing this chapter, it's a beautiful spring day in Austin. I am at my parents' lake house on the shores of Lake Austin. I'm outside with my computer, seated at a picnic table about thirty feet from the water. I had just started typing the first sentence of this paragraph, the one about revelation implying a human recipient ready to receive it, when my cell phone rang. After taking the call, I thought about my phone. It's designed to receive and make calls. It's built for communication. Sure, it can record numbers and display pictures and even play little tunes, but it's still a phone. Its purpose is to enable communication.

Now think about this: how foolish would it be for the research and development department at Nokia to spend millions of dollars producing and marketing a device that had no use? They wouldn't do that. Nokia isn't in the business of inventing cell phones; they're in the business of making cell phones cooler, more exciting, more useful, and more popular. They make cell phones because the need and ability to communicate through the airwaves already exists. The very fact that I'm sitting here with a cell phone nearby presupposes that communication can take place through it. If someone wasn't able to call me, or if I couldn't use it to call others, I'd have no need for it. The phone's ability to receive messages reflects the reality that messages are most likely going to be sent.

Think about your mind. It is perfectly formed to receive revelation. Your brain responds to the stimuli of dreams, ideas, thoughts, visions, and even emotions, and it processes them so their meanings can be known. And if in that processing of information you come to the conclusion that God may, in fact, be trying to tell you something, you've just assumed that you are preequipped to hear from him. Why would you suspect that God was speaking to you if you were not equipped with the capacity to receive his message? You conclude that God is calling because you've been prewired from creation to answer him when he does.

Why have people throughout the ages persistently sought that which was beyond them? Why have thinkers, scholars, and scientists—along with farmers, shepherds, and servants—concluded almost universally that something exists that is bigger, smarter, and even holier than they are? Why is the world today still filled with religious people?

Because there is an eternal homing device built into the mind of every human being. Because our minds are preconditioned to receive spiritual stimuli. Because the "phone" keeps ringing, and our natural, rational, thoughtful instinct is to answer it.

Cultures that embrace the reality of divine revelation are more likely to excel because they understand the radical, eternal truth that they were created for a relationship with something beyond themselves. When you come to the conclusion not just that God exists but that he is, in fact, reaching out to you, then you have just acknowledged that there is more to your meaning and existence than meets the eye. You've responded correctly to the stimuli. You heard the "ring," and you answered.

Why Faith Makes Sense

Faith in God is natural. It is unnatural *not* to believe. The very brain that you use to process whether or not you believe in God couldn't even entertain the possibility of God's existence if he hadn't planted the idea there in the first place. Your mind is set up to be spiritual. It's preprogrammed to search for its Creator. It's the Tranquility Base of the human soul. And when you acknowledge and embrace your spiritual leanings, you're doing what comes naturally.

People who argue that Christianity is a religion for non-thinkers and that it doesn't require any mental effort simply haven't done their homework. When God reveals himself to us, the process always includes a mental component. Christianity isn't for *non*-thinkers. Actually, the opposite is true: Christianity is for *thinkers.* The most common way that people initially discover God is by thinking about him.

Part 2

THE CALL
OF THE WILD

It would be very difficult to explain why the universe should have begun in just this way, except as an act of a God who intended to create beings like us.

Stephen Hawking, scientist

We have had enough of the Darwinian fallacy. It is about time we cry: "The Emperor Has No Clothes."

Kenneth Hsu, geologist

3

Rocky Mountain High

Flattop Mountain. The name says it all. Standing in the front range of the Rocky Mountains about seventy miles northwest of Denver, Flattop is a sloping, gradual climb that levels off to the equivalent of about ten square football fields at just over twelve thousand feet.

To a beginning hiker, Flattop has two big attractions. First, it's relatively easy to climb. A wide trail, beautiful views, a gentle grade, and a short trip to the summit make it the perfect climb for a beginning hiker. Children and adults from all over the world have cut their hiking teeth on Flattop. If someone wants to boast about climbing in the Rockies but needs the path of least resistance, Flattop's their mountain. The second big attraction to Flattop is where it gets you. The mountain itself offers just a routine climb, but it places the adventurous climber in the perfect spot to launch into several hours or several days of mountain hopping.

Flattop was my first real mountain. My dad knew that it would be the perfect climb for his novice son to get initiated into hiking. I was eleven years old when Dad and I packed our bologna sandwiches, laced up our hiking boots, and trekked up Flattop for the first time. We covered the 4.5-mile trail to the summit in about three hours. It was an incredible experience. I literally felt like I had conquered the world. From the summit of Flattop, one gets amazing views—plains to the east, Rockies and Tetons to the north, and more Rockies to the west and south. As I gazed at all of this for the first time, realizing that my own legs had carried me there with little pain and much payoff, I was instantly hooked. I was forever to be a hiker. I was also about to become . . . spiritual.

My dad, wanting to venture out more than his now-trail-weary son, set me on a rock with my sandwich and a bag of Cheetos and took off to climb a nearby taller mountain, Hallet Peak. The summit of Flattop is so wide open that I could actually watch my dad the entire hour that it took him to hike to the summit of Hallet and back. So there I sat, an eleven-year-old kid all alone at twelve thousand feet above sea level, well above timberline, with only the spectacular mountain scenery and the wind to keep me company.

Now, it is important for me to point out that when Dad left me on that rock, he did not say, "Hey, son, I want you to have a religious experience while I'm gone." Actually, I think he said something like, "I'll be gone an hour. You can watch me the whole way. If you need to pee, pick a rock and go for it. Mountains don't care." Certainly not a typical pep talk for a spiritual moment.

But a spiritual moment happened nonetheless. From the summit of Flattop, I had a spectacular view of the fourteen-thousand-foot granddaddy of the Rockies, Longs Peak. Longs is the tallest peak in Rocky Mountain National Park and one of the tallest in Colorado. It is a massive hunk of rock that dwarfs every other mountain in sight. From Flattop,

Longs and its surrounding peaks form what looks like a giant mountain throne, complete with armrests, backrest, and seat. It requires only a little imagination to see a giant mountain monarch taking his place on the Longs throne and ruling over the entire western half of the country. The giant mountain king I met that day was God.

The experience wasn't frightening at all. Rather, it was overwhelming, almost emotional. I remember sitting there, staring at the throne, the only sound in my ears being the wind, and having this powerful sensation that *I was not alone.* There was something personal, something real, something divine, to what I was experiencing. I think that was what made the difference for me: I wasn't just looking at the view, I was experiencing it. There was something—actually, some-*one*—there with me. And I knew, as sure as I sat there alone on that rock, that it was God.

That day on Flattop became a defining moment in my life. It marked me. Before that day, I believed in God and had even been baptized. I had knowledge of the Bible's claims of God, but I can't say that I had ever really experienced him. But that day on Flattop, I did—I tasted him, I felt him, I encountered him—and it changed me forever. Some might say that I was preconditioned by my Sunday school upbringing to interpret the wind as God or to look for him in the beauty of the mountains. I don't think so. I can guarantee you that I was neither thinking of nor looking for God while up on that mountain. Eleven-year-olds, when left to themselves—especially at twelve thousand feet on a wide-open, windy mountain ridge—don't naturally drift toward thinking about God. I sure didn't. It was rather as if something tapped me on the shoulder. It was like I knew I was being watched, but not in a scary way. It was as if I had wandered off course and stumbled onto God's private property, then stumbled onto

God, but he didn't care. Whatever I stumbled onto that day, I have not yet gotten over it.

I have returned to that spot on Flattop several times since then. Each of my children has been there too. It's one of my personal tabernacles. Perhaps you have a few tabernacles of your own.

The Message of Nature

What happened to me on Flattop? What did I encounter that day? Was it altitude sickness? Was it a bad mix of Cheetos and bologna? How did a kid on a rock go from tired hiker to inspired worshiper with no external influence other than the wind and scenery? Was my mind playing tricks on me, or was it reading the obvious signs and coming to logical conclusions? The answer is best expressed in the term *natural revelation.*

Revelation, as we have seen, is an unveiling, a revealing; it is something unknown being made known. It's the mysterious and foggy becoming familiar and clear. In biblical lingo, it's the mystery of God being explained by God himself.

Natural revelation, or *general revelation,* as theologians like to call it, is God introducing himself to people through nature. It's God making his existence obvious, undeniable, and logical through the evidence of nature. When I came to the conclusion that I wasn't alone on that mountain, I was experiencing natural revelation. God pulled back just a bit of the mystery surrounding himself and began the process of making himself known to me, and he used a mountain to do it.

How many times have you slowed your car down to catch an extra long look at a sunset? How often have you lain in your bed at night totally in awe of (and perhaps even fearful of) an intense thunderstorm? How many times have you stood on a beach listening to the pounding waves and had the feeling that they were trying to tell you something? All of that is natural revelation.

Natural revelation comes through our senses and into our brains. It is the opening movement in the symphony of God that plays to the mind of every human being. It happens on a moment-by-moment, hour-by-hour, day-by-day, and season-by-season basis. It is nature doing what it does best: pointing to God. Natural revelation is the entry-level step to knowing God, and every person on earth has experienced it.

So when you feel "inspired" by a sky filled with stars, when you get goose bumps standing at the foot of a seventy-foot mountain waterfall, or when you are so blown away by the intricacies of a tiny ladybug that your natural inclination is not only to believe in God but also to worship him, then you are responding correctly. Your mind has accurately processed the mental stimuli. The skeptics and atheists of the world have it backward: it's not unreasonable to look at a sunset and conclude there is a God; it's unreasonable to look at a sunset and conclude there is not one.

Take a Look Around

The apostle Paul was no mental lightweight. He saw no disconnect between having a profound faith and having a profound intellect. For Paul, it was reasonable to believe in God because nature made an irrefutable case for his existence. In fact, when given the opportunity to address a group of scholars and philosophers in Athens, Paul talked to them about the overwhelming evidence of natural revelation. Consider what he said to them:

Men of Athens! I see that in every way you are very religious. For as I walked around and looked carefully at your objects of worship, I even found an altar with this inscription: TO AN UNKNOWN GOD. Now what you worship as something unknown I am going to proclaim to you. The God who made the world and everything in it is the Lord of heaven and earth and does not live in temples built by hands. And he is not served by human hands, as if he needed anything, because he himself gives all men life and breath and everything else. From one man he made every nation of men, that they should inhabit the whole earth; and he determined the times set for them and the exact places where they should live. God did this so that men would seek him and perhaps reach out for him and find him, though he is not far from each one of us.

Acts 17:22–27

Do you see what Paul did there? To help identify God to this highly informed group of thinkers, Paul used a line of reasoning he felt they were sure to understand. He argued that there was something obviously great and powerful behind nature and the created world. He asked them to acknowledge it. He basically said, "Hey, guys, you're smart and well read, but you're missing the obvious. This 'unknown God' that you acknowledge isn't unknown at all. Take a look around. Where do you think this world came from? You know it has a source. The God of the universe made everything you can see. Every breath you take is from him. He's the God of all creation, and he fully expects you to worship him."

Paul believed that he was on solid ground in arguing for the reality of a holy God from the evidence of the created world. He felt that the power of natural revelation was so strong, so magnetic, and so persuasive that anyone—even the most sophisticated thinkers—would be foolish to deny it. He was right. Listen to the witness of the biblical writers:

- David: "The heavens declare the glory of God; the skies proclaim the work of his hands. Day after day they pour forth speech; night after night they display knowledge. There is no speech or language where their voice is not heard" (Ps. 19:1–3).

- Job: "But ask the animals, and they will teach you, or the birds of the air, and they will tell you; or speak to the earth, and it will teach you, or let the fish of the sea inform you. Which of all these does not know that the hand of the LORD has done this? In his hand is the life of every creature and the breath of all mankind" (Job 12:7–10).

- Isaiah: "Lift your eyes and look to the heavens: Who created all these? He who brings out the starry host one by one, and calls them each by name. Because of his great power and mighty strength, not one of them is missing" (Isa. 40:26).

- The writer of Hebrews: "For every house is built by someone, but God is the builder of everything" (Heb. 3:4).

I could list several other biblical writers. But here's the point: many of these writers, including Paul, the greatest Christian apologist of all time, reasoned that the reality of God's existence was obvious. Based on the evidence of the natural world, belief in God was the most logical conclusion at which a thinking person could arrive.

Do the Math

So is it possible, even logical, for a thinking person to believe that God created the world around us? If so, that person is in good company. Did you know that many of the greatest scientific minds in the world find belief in God to be reasonable, logical, and consistent with the scientific evidence? Consider what some scholars have said:

- Michael Behe, biochemist at Lehigh University: "The result of these cumulative efforts to investigate the cell—to investigate life at the molecular level—is a loud, clear piercing cry of 'design!'"[1]
- Professor E. W. F. Tomlin, chair of philosophy and literature at the University of Nice—"To ascribe their [the brain and the nervous system] development to the play of blind forces is to suspend rational judgment and to betray the cause of science."[2]
- James Tour, professor in the department of chemistry in the Center for Nanoscale Science and Technology at Rice University: "I stand in awe of God because of what He has done through His creation. Only a rookie who knows nothing about science would say science takes away from faith. If you really study science, it will bring you closer to God."[3]
- Alan Hayward, physicist: "The case for the existence of the Creator is stronger today than it ever has been. In every branch of science there is a growing body of evidence that the universe's contents have been *designed*—that things just could not be the way they are as the result of chance."[4]
- Fred Heeren, cosmologist: "Logic leads us to believe that the First Cause [the source for the universe and all life in it] must be separate from what it created, transcending it—that it must be eternal, spiritual, all-powerful, all-knowing, purposing tremendous undertakings on behalf of human beings, personal—in short, that this First Cause is more perfectly explained by the God of the Bible than by anything else."[5]

- Robert Jastrow, astronomer: "For the scientist who has lived by his faith in the power of reason, the story ends like a bad dream. He has scaled the mountains of ignorance; he is about to conquer the highest peaks; as he pulls himself over the final rock, he is greeted by a band of theologians who have been seated there for centuries."[6]

Aren't these some amazing statements? It's too bad that such comments don't get more airtime. I hope they encourage you. I hope they rally you to stop apologizing for what you believe. Whenever you hear of a scientist, a scholar, or a philosopher criticizing believers for being unscientific, remember those statements. There are numerous well-trained scientists, biologists, cosmologists, geologists, astronomers, and even philosophers who find faith in God to be quite reasonable. So remind yourself that your faith isn't foolish. You haven't lost your mind. In fact, you're using it.

Why Faith Makes Sense

Creation stands as a witness to the reality of God every minute of every day. It tells us that the evidence for God is so undeniable and so irrefutable that each of us is actually accountable to God for our response to him.[7] Most Americans, it seems, are getting the message. Despite the airtime they get, those who truly don't believe in God still represent only about 10 percent of the American population.[8] That means that if you are open to the reality of God, not only are you among the vast majority of Americans, but at least partly your response to the message of nature has placed you there. How's that for the ultimate irony? You find yourself in the belief camp because you *did* listen to reason.

4

Tracks in the Snow

.

A few years ago, while snowshoeing high in the Rocky Mountains in the middle of winter, I came upon a fresh set of cat tracks. There in the snow before me were huge paw prints spread evenly on alternating sides. When I say huge, I mean *HUGE*. I made a fist with my gloved hand and stuck it in one of the prints without touching any of the snow surrounding the track. My fist fit inside the perimeter of the print.

That's when I started doing the mental math. Not of how big this cat was or of how fast it was likely to run—I knew I was outgunned by such a majestic animal. No, I started doing the math on when the tracks might have been made. It was now about noon. I had been snowshoeing in the woods without a trail for about two hours. It had snowed nonstop for the last twenty-four hours. Several inches of fresh powder covered anything on the ground that hadn't been left there recently—quite recently. In other words, these tracks had been made sometime between the early morning hours and right then. They couldn't have been more than just a few hours old. Which meant that not too long before I had trekked through those woods, a very large mountain lion had done the exact same thing—only she had four paws, a fur coat, and a distinct home-field advantage. And I had no idea if she had passed that spot minutes or hours before.

I decided to leave. I had no desire to meet Mrs. Mountain Lion out in those woods, especially with a cumbersome tennis-racket contraption strapped to each foot. So I simply pivoted a full 180 degrees and started to walk back the way I had come. That's when I heard it: *GRRRRrrrrrrrr*. I'm sure my heart stopped beating. From the direction of a nearby ridge, I heard a distinct, low-pitched growl. It terrified me. I didn't see anything move or detect any sign of the cat. But I had no doubt that I had heard her growl, and I assumed she was growling at me. I stood absolutely still for about ten minutes. I was scared to even draw a significant breath. I knew that any sudden movement on my part might bring out Mrs. Cat and all of her furred fury.

Ten minutes later I decided to move again. I had heard no other cat sounds during my frozen standoff, which I found encouraging. But I knew I couldn't stay there indefinitely, so I decided to take my chances that the big cat had lost interest in me. I took a step—nothing happened. Whew! I took two more—still nothing. I took my fourth step—*GRRRRrrrrrrrr*. There she was again, still growling from just behind the ridge. Now I knew I was in real trouble.

I thought about the hunting knife in my backpack. If I could get to it, I might at least have a fighting chance. I had determined that standing still wasn't doing me any good. Mama Cat seemed to be just toying with me, so I dropped my pack off my shoulder and started digging for my knife. I thought that maybe all of my jerky movements would scare the cat off. Then, *GRRRRrrrrrrr*. Then another, but higher-pitched *GGGRRRRrrrrrrr*. And then, *GGGRRRRrrrrrrr uttttuuuummmmm*. . . . It was a jackhammer. Somewhere behind the nearby ridge, down in the valley, at least a half mile away, a construction worker was punching a hole in concrete with a loud, air-powered jackhammer, and I had mistaken it for a mountain lion.

Talk about relieved. I laughed all the way back down the mountain. I was giddy to still be in one piece and not be fighting a mountain lion with a hunting knife and stupid snowshoes. I also found it rather humorous that, after seeing those cat tracks, I had somehow managed to interpret the distant, low roar of a jackhammer as the mountain lion growling at me from just over the ridge. I had seen one set of signs (the tracks) and then wrongly concluded that the subsequent signs (the sounds) were related to the first. It was an easy mistake to make, but a mistake nonetheless.

Drawing the Right Conclusion

That's precisely the mistake that our culture accuses believers of making when they interpret the "signs" in nature as evidence of God. You see tracks everywhere, tracks that appear to have been made by a creating God. You see the tracks in an ocean sunrise. You see the tracks in the miracle of a newborn baby. You see the tracks in a field of wildflowers and in the steady changing of the seasons. Look at an orca whale, and you'll see God-prints. Watch the amazing aerial acrobatics of a common butterfly, and you'll see God-prints. Study the hovering abilities of a hummingbird, and you'll once again see God-prints.

And like cat tracks in the mountain snow, when you see prints all around you that could only have been left by an awesome, creating God, it just makes sense to conclude that God made them.

Then, after you see all this, you hear something. While examining the tracks and contemplating what kind of awesome being could create a moon, control the wind, or design a parakeet, you hear something. Deep in your mind, in the regions of your brain where you process all things logical and reasonable, you hear something. It's not a voice, but it's a message nonetheless. Your mind is sending a signal to the rest of your consciousness. You are reaching a conclusion about what you've seen. Synapses are firing, electrons are flowing, your brain is functioning. You find yourself thinking about words and phrases such as *obvious, no doubt, irrefutable, the evidence clearly indicates, of course,* and *it's simple, really.* Then, like an eleven-year-old left alone on a mountain summit, you conclude, *These tracks were made by God.* And you know what? You're right. Your mind has led you to the obvious conclusion: only God could do something like this.

You've encountered the source, what William Paley first described in 1802 as the watchmaker. Paley argued that if you discover a watch lying on the beach, and you examine its intricately moving and perfectly aligned parts, you logically conclude that the watch has a maker. Nothing so precise or finely tuned ever just happens. In the same way, argued Paley, the universe and the intricacies of human life obviously point to a designer/creator. Nearly 1,500 years earlier, Aristotle had drawn the same conclusion, describing God as the "Unmoved Mover," or the unchanging source to all life and matter in the universe. Both of these thinkers reasoned that if something looks designed and acts designed, chances are it *is* designed. You see tracks in the snow, and you think, *Something made those.*

Oh, that it were so simple. As you know, you are not left to think about God in a cultural vacuum. The minute you conclude with your mind that God is the great track maker, our culture comes along and tells you that you're mistaken. You read that there are natural, tangible, and measurable explanations for everything. You're told that science can indeed explain every effect by a series of small causes that have nothing to do with the divine. You're rebuked and criticized for allowing such a magnificent machine as your mind to become so undisciplined that it actually succumbs to the tomfoolery of religious belief. You're told that you haven't heard God at all, and that you, like me on the Rocky Mountains, have misinterpreted what you are hearing.

But you haven't. Stop right now and tell yourself that you're not foolish for concluding that only a creating God could make all that we see around us. Tell yourself that your mind has not misled you and that you have not reached an illogical conclusion. Because, dear friend, unlike the mixed message of fresh cat tracks in the snow and the distant rumble of a jackhammer, God's signals are never mixed. When you gaze at the beauty of a daffodil or stand in awe of the raw power of a thunderstorm, when your mind tells you that it is logical to conclude that only an awesome God could create such things, and when your heart tells you that it is therefore appropriate to bow in worship before such a God, *you are not confused at all.* Those are the exact conclusions that nature was designed to help you reach. You have correctly interpreted the message; you would have to set aside reason and logic to conclude otherwise.

Tell Me What You See

Some of the most sobering words on this subject in the Bible are found in the first chapter of Romans. We've already established that Paul, the author of Romans and many other New Testament letters, was a thinker and scholar of the highest order. He was a profoundly intellectual man who found faith in God to be quite rational. He had no problem looking into the eyes of the greatest thinkers and philosophers of his day and calling them to believe. In Romans 1, Paul wrote what is arguably the Bible's definitive statement on the implications and significance of natural revelation: "The wrath of God is being revealed from heaven against all the godlessness and wickedness of men who suppress the truth by their wickedness, since what may be known about God is plain to them, because God has made it plain to them. For since the creation of the world God's invisible qualities—his eternal power and divine nature—have been clearly seen, being understood from what has been made, so that men are without excuse" (Rom. 1:18–20). I've read those words countless times, and they still take my breath away. Let's consider the weight of what Paul was saying.

He began with an unpopular subject—God's wrath. Paul claimed that God's anger is actually being poured out from heaven because of humanity's outright, blatant suppression of God's truth. This suppression happens when people deny and reject what should be obvious to them about God. Paul argued that what can be known about God, what he has chosen to reveal, is plain to every human through the evidence in nature. Paul didn't say that we can know everything about God—there are still many things we don't know about him, things we will learn only in eternity—but he did say that there is plenty about God we can know and be sure of. In other words, God never reveals anything in a confusing way.

When God reveals a truth about himself, he does so in a way that is undeniable. His revelation can be rejected, but not ignored. There is no way it can be missed by the human mind.

According to Paul, God, through his creative work in nature, made his existence obvious, his reality undeniable. In a beautiful play on words, Paul argued that the *invisible* realities of God—specifically, his eternal power and divine nature—were made *visible* through the created world. Even though we can't see God, we can learn much about him just by looking at the world around us. We can reach the correct conclusions about God and nature just by studying his creation. Nature, it seems, is there to help us understand and worship the invisible God.

Take our universe as an example. Scientists' best guess today is that the universe is between twelve and fifteen billion years old. So whatever caused the universe, whatever got it started, has to pre-date the universe's date of origin. Look up into the heavens and know that God preceded everything you see. Through the stars, nature reveals God's eternal power. When God kick-started the universe into existence, he did so from the standpoint of eternity, not time. He has never been bound by time. In fact, time is something God created. The Bible says that God's eternal power is inarguable, inescapable, and undeniable, just based on the reality of the stars that we see each night (see Pss. 19:1–4; 97:6).

Paul also taught that creation reflects God's divine nature. He said that only a creating God, only the ultimate divine source of all things, could do something as splendid and majestic as what we see above and around us.

Think again about our universe. Do you know how big it is? Well, we can measure only the parts of it we can see. If the universe is fifteen billion years old, then its size today is the same as the distance light travels in fifteen billion years (i.e., fifteen billion light-years). The speed of light is 186,000 miles per second. If you want to get a picture of how big the universe is, multiply 186,000 by the number of seconds in a year (31,536,000), then multiply that number times fifteen billion, then put the word *miles* behind your answer, and you'll get an idea of just how far the universe reaches. And that's just the part we can see. But wait, we're not done. Our universe is expanding! It's actually increasing in diameter, much like ripples on the surface of a pond spread out and expand.

We know from physics that an effect is never greater than its cause. For every measurable effect, there is an equal or greater cause. If you find a size 12 shoe print in the sand (effect), you can draw some logical conclusions about the size of the shoe that made it (cause). If the effect is a hole in a wall the size of a fist, you can logically conclude something about its cause. Similarly, if the effect is an expanding universe that's currently fifteen billion light-years in diameter, what can we logically conclude about its cause? We conclude, quite simply, that its cause is powerful enough to produce something like our universe. Furthermore, it would be illogical to conclude that our universe had no source at all. Why should we believe those who tell us that our perfectly functioning universe—a universe that is precisely fitted for life on our planet—is a great cosmic accident? That's not logical. In fact, it takes more faith to believe that such a grand universe is an accident than to believe it's the work of a creating God. When you gaze up into the heavens and have your faith in God confirmed yet again, you are reaching the exact conclusion that you should be. You're being neither unreasonable nor illogical. You're simply agreeing with the testimony of the evidence that's before you.

No Excuses

There is one final phrase in Paul's treatise on creation in Romans 1 that we need to note, and it may be the most sobering point of all. After telling us that the truth of God is plainly evident, after saying that God's invisible attributes—his eternal power and divine nature—can be clearly seen through creation, and after arguing that nature makes an irrefutable case for the existence of God, Paul adds a chilling phrase: "so that men are without excuse" (Rom. 1:20). God does not seem to think that the matter of his existence is open to interpretation.

So convincing is the evidence for the reality of God, so overwhelming is the argument made from the created world, and so obvious is the source of natural revelation, that humans are deemed accountable for the information that nature contains. Based on what Paul argues, we must come to the rather troubling conclusion that it is impossible for people to misinterpret the evidence for God; they can only deny it. Worse, according to Romans 1, they suppress it. The profound evidence of nature works in tandem with the hardwiring of your mind to lead you to the conclusion that God is real. Belief in a holy God is not one interpretation of many that the evidence of nature might produce; it is the only interpretation that is logical. So logical, in fact, that God considers it fair and just to hold humans accountable for their response to the message that the created world communicates. To look at the tracks in the snow and the prints left all over the world by our all-powerful, creative source, and then to proclaim that God doesn't exist—that isn't smart, it's foolish.

Consider the poetic witness of the Old Testament writers:

Dominion and awe belong to God;
    he establishes order in the heights of heaven.

Job 25:2

For all the gods of the nations are idols,
    but the Lord made the heavens.

Psalm 96:5

The heavens proclaim his righteousness,
    and all the peoples see his glory.

Psalm 97:6

The Lord has made his salvation known
    and revealed his righteousness to the nations.

Psalm 98:2

You turn things upside down,
    as if the potter were thought to be like the clay!
Shall what is formed say to him who formed it,
    "He did not make me"?
Can the pot say of the potter,
    "He knows nothing"?

Isaiah 29:16

It is I who made the earth
    and created mankind upon it.
My own hands stretched out the heavens;
    I marshaled their starry hosts.

Isaiah 45:12

What Nature Is Saying to You and Me

Trying to ignore the messages about God through nature is like trying to ignore the grizzly bear that's rummaging around outside your tent: it's neither wise nor possible. Let's consider the implications of this first level of exposure to God that we all have through natural revelation.

First, *natural revelation makes belief in God rational.* The logical conclusion to the evidence around us is that everything is the work of a designing God. The laws of cause and effect require us to consider the great cause that alone could produce such an awesome effect as our world and universe. Only something bigger and more powerful could be responsible for such grandeur. Our list of plausible possibilities is short indeed. Theologians and philosophers call this the argument of First Cause, and it can be traced all the way back to Plato and Aristotle. Try as they may, scientists have a difficult time answering what this First Cause could be without making at least some veiled reference to something divine. Natural revelation argues that the evidence for God isn't just overwhelming, it's conclusive.

Second, *natural revelation implies that all humans have the opportunity to know God.* Humanity's exposure to the reality of God shown through nature is universal. Every person—regardless of the period of history in which he or she lives, regardless of his or her culture, language, religious influence, education, and social status—is exposed to the inarguable evidence of God in nature. No human will ever need to or be able to claim that he or she didn't have a chance to know God. Every person with a functioning mind hears the universal language spoken by the elements of nature (see Ps. 19:1). Every person sees the evidence. Every person is led to the same conclusion. Therefore, every person is given ample opportunity to acknowledge God.

Finally, *those who deny the truth of God are still account-able to him*. The evidence for God cannot be misunder-stood. It can be rejected, denied, or suppressed, but not misinterpreted. Our minds are prewired to both receive and correctly interpret the messages of God sent to us via the natural world. Those messages can be rejected, like block-ing an email from an unwanted sender, but they can't be misread. As a result, God holds all people accountable to him for their response to natural revelation—even if they don't have missionaries, even if they don't have Bibles, even if they are raised in a totally pagan, unbelieving culture. The evidence of God in what they see and encounter in nature is irrefutable. It's strong enough to lead them to the conclu-sion that God is not only real but also holy and worthy of worship, despite their inbred opposing teachings, cultural influences, and religious notions. The words of Paul in Ro-mans 1:18–20 ring true for every human being in history. Because of the sheer power and clarity of natural revelation, we are all without excuse before God.

This is a frightening point to consider for all those who boast that God doesn't exist. Many in our culture are fond of saying that God is out of a job or that he is a figment of our imaginations. But such rhetoric begs a larger question: what's the payoff for arguing against God's existence? Sure, in today's world you might sell some books and make the talk-show circuit. But in the big scheme of things, I don't see the benefit of betting against God.

French mathematician and philosopher Blaise Pascal (1623–1662) made the same point in a much more profound way. In his now-famous argument known as Pascal's Wager, Pascal pointed out the ultimate futility of arguing against God, especially in the face of such overwhelming evidence of his existence. Pascal's Wager goes something like this:

- We cannot prove that God doesn't exist.
- Based on the evidence, it is much more likely that he does exist than that he does not.
- The implications of God's existence are far greater than the implications of his nonexistence.
- Given such high stakes, it is wiser to assume and live as if God does exist than as if he does not.

In other words, "Dude, I don't know about you, but I'm betting on God."

What's the bottom line? You've got much more to gain by leaning into your belief in God, even if you still have major doubts, than you do by rejecting him. The two-thousand-year-old wisdom of the New Testament says that your heart is telling you the truth. Pascal had stern words for those who try to deny God: "Before entering into the proofs of the Christian religion, I find it necessary to point out the sinfulness of those men who live in indifference to the search for truth in a matter which is so important to them, and which touches them so nearly."[1] Perhaps King David said it best over three thousand years ago: "The fool says in his heart, 'There is no God'" (Ps. 53:1).

Why Faith Makes Sense

Does this make your blood flow just a little faster? You don't need to feel foolish or uninformed for believing in an awesome, creating God. The next time you feel the wind in your face, listen to a gentle rain, smell salty sea air or the freshness of a spring flower, stand transfixed before a California redwood, or look at the curious design of a praying mantis, remember that you have no reason not to be a worshiper. In the same way you would walk up to an artist and say, "That is really beautiful. Way to go," you can kneel before the creating force behind all that's out there (God) and say, "That is really beautiful. I worship you." And the next time you're on a mountain and you find your arms covered with goose bumps, the hair standing up on the back of your neck, and your heart strangely warmed, remember, you're not alone up there. You never have been.

5

How Did We Get Here?

In 6th grade I had a very influential teacher, a Jewish man named Mr. Meyer, who was very passionate about learning. His knowledge and personal style really appealed to my budding intellectual instincts. The year was 1974—the year I stopped being a Christ-follower. In fact, to my parents' chagrin, I declared myself an atheist after sitting through Mr. Meyer's lengthy series of science lectures on Darwinism and evolutionary theory.

The lectures pulled no punches. He clearly denounced any other thinking as being childlike or fantasy-based. From my "twelve-year-old who wants to believe anything his teacher says" perspective, he made an airtight case for evolution. After 12 years of going to church with my family, I pushed back hard against them. I stopped attending and believing.

My parents weren't in a great position to defend against the "scientific" argument I learned in school. They didn't know the counterclaims and weren't particularly scholarly concerning Old Testament teachings. My line of reasoning was something along the lines that if you couldn't believe the first chapter of the Bible, how could you confidently believe the rest of it? It was a difficult position to argue against—even with a 12-year-old.[1]

Those words were written by Dave, who serves as an elder in the church I pastor. He is a bright, articulate, and successful entrepreneur with a Harvard MBA. He is also now a committed Christ-follower. But as you can tell, his journey to faith hasn't been easy. In an all-too-familiar story, his desire to believe was overruled by his need to know. Faith lost out to "fact," and religion surrendered to "intelligence." Dave's belief in God was dethroned by a common foe to religious belief and the most frequently cited argument for embracing good old-fashioned atheism: Darwin's theory of evolution.

Some of you may have finished the last chapter thinking, *But what about evolution? You said that the evidence for God is overwhelming because of nature, but science tells us that evolution explains nature and even human existence. How do you account for that? How can you believe in a creating God when much of science claims there isn't one?*

I'm glad you asked.

Just the Facts, Ma'am

The corporate embrace of evolution as fact, not theory, by government, universities, and, of course, many in the scientific community has given spiritual skeptics much to cheer about and much ammunition with which to bombard believers. You have no doubt read countless articles and cover stories in *Time, Newsweek, Psychology Today, U.S. News and World Report, USA Today,* the *New York Times,* the *Washington Post*, and the *Wall Street Journal*, citing discovery after discovery proving the case for randomness and driving yet another nail in the coffin of God. According to conventional wisdom, belief in God is no longer necessary or respectable. In today's skeptically minded culture, God is no longer in the picture; evolution is the reason why.

Richard Dawkins is an Oxford zoologist who is perhaps the world's foremost authority on and defender of Darwin's theory of evolution. He is also an outspoken atheist. He once gave a lecture entitled "A Scientist's Case against God." Dawkins isn't concerned about who he offends when it comes to arguing the illegitimacy of all religious faith. That which makes faith ultimately obsolete, according to Dawkins, is the fact of evolution: "One thing all real scientists agree upon is the fact of evolution itself. It is a fact that we are cousins of gorillas, kangaroos, starfish, and bacteria. Evolution is as much a fact as the heat of the sun. It is not a theory, and for pity's sake, let's stop confusing the philosophically naive by calling it so. Evolution is a fact."[2]

Such rhetoric can be more than a little intimidating. Has all of science really concluded that our roots lie in the accidental processes of evolution and not in the mind of a creating God? The answer is a resounding NO. Did you know that over seven hundred scientists from around the world have formed an organization that calls into question the scientific legitimacy of Darwinism and evolutionary theory? Their "Scientific Dissent from Darwinism" expresses their skepticism over "the ability of Darwinian theory to account for life as we know it."[3] It is signed by scientists from the US National Academy of Sciences; from Russian, Hungarian, and Czech national academies; and from universities such as Yale, Princeton, Stanford, MIT, UC Berkeley, UCLA, and others. A similar statement of dissent has been published by medical doctors.

Despite the ongoing media barrage declaring evolution's supremacy, Westerners remain unconvinced. In the past twenty years, the percentage of Americans who believe in evolution has fallen from 45 to 40 percent.[4] According to atheist Sam Harris, "Only 28% of Americans believe in evolution (and two-thirds of these believe evolution was 'guided by God'). 53% [of Americans] are actually creationists."[5] If you find yourself a little hesitant to believe that the marvels of our world are accidental, be encouraged—you're not alone. You're in the majority.

The reality is that a great number of thinking believers and even unbelievers simply do not put stock in the credibility of evolutionary theory. But tragically, many of us in the Christian community are so intimidated by the fine print of Darwinism and by the strident tone of those who try to discredit belief that we feel we have no capacity to engage Dawkins, Harris, or those who agree with them in meaningful dialogue. We are afraid, quite honestly, that we will have our heads and our theology handed to us on a platter.

We won't. But we also can't charge in unprepared. So let's review some basics about evolution.[6]

Evolution 101

Here are a few terms and names that will help you better grasp the basics in the discussion about evolution and creation.

- *Evolution.* In its broadest sense, evolution refers to the natural processes by which things in nature adapt and change. For example, viruses have an uncanny ability to become resistant to antibiotics that were once highly effective against them. Sequential generations of birds have been shown to change feather colors or beak sizes as they adapt to the challenges of their environment. Whenever you see nature adapting or changing, basic evolution is at work. Such changes that we see every day in nature are normal and are consistent with the Bible's description of how God created the world. (We'll discuss this further later.)

- *Charles Darwin* (1809–1882). Darwin was a British naturalist who first proposed a scientific theory of how life could have evolved. He spent five years traveling aboard the *HMS Beagle,* studying adaptive patterns in nature. The changes he observed in nature led him to conclude that all life might have originated from one original, microscopic source. Darwin proposed his theory in his landmark book *The Origin of Species* in 1859. Although Darwin was raised in the Church of England and even studied to be a clergyman, it is believed that he died an agnostic.

- *Darwinism.* Darwin's theory of evolution in its twenty-first-century version states that all forms of life evolved from one original speck of microscopic bacteria, and that the evolutionary process that produced such life was not guided by any overseeing or divine power. In other words, it was all completely random. Darwin coined the phrases *natural selection* and *survival of the fittest* to describe how he believed evolution occurred. He taught that every species of life, in order to survive, had to evolve and adapt. Nature singled out for extinction those species that were not able to evolve or adapt, and it selected for survival those that were. The phrases *singled out* and *selected* may seem to imply that

73

a divine power was guiding the process, but they are not meant to. Darwinism stands firm in the belief that the work done in nature through evolution was completely random and accidental, resulting in all the life-forms that we see today, including humans. Many scientists believe that Darwin's theory is a satisfactory explanation of how life came to be and that no need exists for a divine being to start and/or guide the process.

- *Microevolution.* Microevolution is evolution, or change, that occurs on a small scale. It occurs only within a certain species. What Darwin observed on his five-year study aboard the *Beagle* was microevolution. When a finch's wings change colors or a fruit fly's wings adjust in size, that's microevolution. When breeders create a new breed of cat through crossbreeding, it's microevolution, albeit helped along by humans. Microevolution allows for cats to adapt and evolve, but it doesn't allow them to become something other than cats. They might have bigger paws or keener eyesight, but they're still part of the cat family. Microevolution is supported by the bulk of fossil and archaeological evidence and is consistent with the biblical record of creation in Genesis.[7]

- *Macroevolution.* Macroevolution is evolution, or change, that occurs on a large scale. It is change so dramatic that it yields a new species. Macroevolution is portrayed perfectly in the educational cartoons that show a fish swimming around and then sprouting legs and crawling up on the shore, thus becoming a reptile. Later, that same reptile sprouts wings and flies away, becoming a bird. Macroevolution teaches that all life can be traced back to one original form and that there are no hard boundaries fixed around species. In other words, there are no fixed genetic limits for what a species can evolve into, given enough time. In macroevolution, bacteria become fish, fish become reptiles, reptiles become mammals, and mammals become humans. And all of this happens through an infinite number of accidents and birth variations. Darwin did not observe macroevolution; in fact, no one has, as it theoretically takes hundreds of millions of years. Darwin observed microevolution (small changes) and concluded that macroevolution (large changes) was possible. There is only a small amount of physical fossil and archaeological evidence that appears to support the claim of macroevolution. Macroevolution is also inconsistent with the Bible's teachings about creation in Genesis. (Later I will give arguments against the scientific viability and logic of macroevolution, also called *Darwinian evolution*.)

- *Theistic evolution.* Theistic evolution teaches that God created the world through macroevolution. It combines the belief in God as Creator with the overarching evolutionary claims that all life can be traced to some original life-form. While theistic evolution makes a noble effort at bringing the worlds of science and theology together, thinkers on both sides of the issue have registered strong objections to its claims.

- *The Big Bang.* First proposed in 1927 and later verified in 1965, Big Bang science teaches that our universe began as a microscopic piece of cosmic matter that erupted and eventually expanded into the universe that we observe today. There is overwhelming scientific evidence to support the idea of a sudden, instantaneous start to our universe. Scientists who study the Big Bang—many of whom are not believers—have been hard-pressed not to reference God when describing the source that could produce such a massive, powerful beginning to the universe. There are no apparent inconsistencies with the belief that the universe started with a big bang and the claim of Genesis that God created the universe out of nothing.

- *Intelligent Design* (ID). Intelligent Design is a relatively new spin on the classic evolution/creation debate. While not completely in the camp of Genesis creationism, ID does argue that the complexity and sophistication of many organisms and species in nature prove that they could not have evolved on a macro scale. Only an intelligent designer could create such complex living organisms. While ID made some initial progress through political inroads (some school boards and colleges have added ID studies to their scientific curriculum), the jury is still out on whether or not it will have any lasting impact in the scientific community.

- *Creationism.* Creationism, as the name implies, argues that life can be accounted for only by the record of human origins presented in the first two chapters of Genesis. Creationists differ on the age of the earth and the universe, their disagreement hinging on the interpretation of the word *day* mentioned in Genesis 1–2. (The literal Hebrew noun can speak of a twenty-four-hour period, but it could also mean *ages, seasons,* and *eons.*) But creationists do agree that the overall point of the Genesis account is that God is the source of all life, that he created all life and matter from nothing, and that he did not use macroevolution as part of the process.

These definitions give you a basic understanding of some of the discussion points in the evolution/creation debate.

While the study of evolution is an incredibly complex science, you don't need a PhD in biology or quantum physics to be able to grasp its basic concepts. Darwinism's claim that all life can be accounted for by random, unguided processes will eventually collide with the voices of logic, reason, and faith. If the claims that all life—despite its beauty, precision, and complexity—can be explained without any reference to a divine Creator seem absurd, perhaps it's because they are.

Six Important Realities

Now that we've learned some of the common vocabulary used in the evolution/creation discussion, let's look at six realities that present significant hurdles evolutionary theory isn't likely to overcome.

Reality #1—Probability. The likelihood of all life randomly evolving into the intricate and sophisticated levels that we now observe is not just statistically improbable, it's also statistically impossible. If you turned in a scientific thesis at a major university with the same odds of failure that macroevolution would have had to overcome in order to occur, you'd be flunked on the spot. This is an area of great hypocrisy for many scientists, because no other theory with such obvious statistical downsides would ever get serious airtime. Yet evolution does, simply because it seems like the best *material* explanation for all existence. If someone is committed to finding an observable and measurable source for life, then evolution has to be right, odds or no odds.

What are the odds? Well, the chances are better—hundreds, thousands, even millions of times better—of you playing *and winning* the lottery every Wednesday and Saturday *for the rest of your life* than of evolving in the random way that evolution claims. Put it all together—the miracle of DNA, the eye, the brain, taste buds, skin, red and white blood cells, the human kidney, the human heart, our planet's tilt and orbit, our exact distance from the sun, gravity, the ozone, a bird's ability to fly, a fly's even greater ability to fly, water's evaporation into the atmosphere, the perfectly functioning snout of an anteater, photosynthesis, and so on. By the time you run the odds of not just one of those things randomly occurring, but all of them randomly coming together as we observe, you'd have a much better chance of jumping out of an airplane from ten thousand feet—without a parachute—and living.

Let me give you a simple example. The living cells that make up humans consist of amino acids and protein molecules. Amino acids, when ordered in the correct way, produce protein molecules. It takes 100 rightly aligned amino acids to make just one protein molecule, and it takes 200 protein molecules to get just one living cell. Do you know what the odds are of just 1 protein molecule (100 amino acids aligned correctly) developing randomly? Try 1 out of every 10—then put 60 zeros behind that 10. In other words, the chances of 1 protein molecule developing randomly are 1 in 10 to the 60th power.[8] And remember, that's just 1 molecule. You need 200 of them to get just 1 living cell.

Add to that the improbability of the earth having just the right kind of galaxy and being in the correct place in that galaxy for life to develop, having the right kind of sun and being precisely the correct distance from that sun, and having the right planetary mass and the right atmosphere, and you begin to see just how statistically impossible evolution really is. Suffice it to say that countless miracles or a several-billion-year run of really good luck would have to "just happen" in order for evolution to be true.

Reality #2—First Cause. I introduced you earlier to the argument of First Cause, and we need to revisit it here. This is clearly the most critical argument in the evolution/creation debate, and the one that atheists have no answer for. It simply asks the question, "Where did the speck come from?" Or, perhaps with a bit more sophistication, "Who or what created that first atom of nonliving, microscopic matter that evolved into all life as we know it?" It's a great question, and one that true evolutionists have to dodge, shrug their shoulders at, or credit aliens with, because they have no other good answer. Matter can't produce itself, and something has to account for the first piece of cosmic matter that evolutionists believe grew into all life as we know it.

Maybe you've heard this one:

God is sitting in heaven when a scientist says to him, "God, we don't need you anymore. Science has finally figured out a way to create life out of nothing!"

"Is that so? Tell me," God replies.

"Well," the scientist says, "we can take dirt, form it into the likeness of a man, and breathe life into it, thus creating man."

"That's very interesting. Show me," God says. So the scientist bends down to the ground and begins to mold the soil into the shape of a man.

"No, no, no," God interrupts. "Get your own dirt."

Or, perhaps better said, "In the beginning God created the heavens and the earth" (Gen. 1:1).

Reality #3—Insufficient evidence. The fossil record is the closest thing we have to an actual photograph or document of how life developed on earth. Interestingly, the fossil record has been and remains one of the weakest links in the chain of evolutionary theory. If Darwin's theory is true—if life on earth gradually evolved over billions of years—then the fossil record should reflect a slow, gradual development of species.

But in reality, it shows the opposite. The fossil record indicates that life started instantaneously and with great diversity of complete, intact species from the outset.

This lack of fossil support wasn't lost on Darwin. After the release of *The Origin of Species*, his most outspoken critics were not theologians but fossil experts, who cited the lack of fossil evidence for his theory.[9] Darwin himself acknowledged the problem. He wrote, "Why, if species have descended from other species . . . do we not see everywhere innumerable transitional forms? Why is not all nature in confusion [in the fossil record] instead of the species being, as we see them, well defined?"[10] Even with nearly a century and a half of archaeological work since the publication of *The Origin of Species*, and with the exception of a few discoveries that might be interpreted as transitional forms, the story the fossils tell remains basically unchanged. And the story they tell is of a sudden explosion of life on earth, not of gradual evolution. Phillip Johnson summed up the fossil issue well in his book *Darwin on Trial*: "If evolution means the gradual change of one kind of organism into another kind, the outstanding characteristic of the fossil record is the absence of evidence for evolution."[11]

Reality #4—Insufficient time. Evolutionists frequently argue that given enough time—read, billions of years—all life as we know it could have randomly evolved. The problem with their reasoning is that the earth simply hasn't been around long enough for macroevolution to occur. Most scientists believe that the earth is only about five billion years old. If that is true—and no one is seriously suggesting that the earth is any older than that—then the evolutionary mechanism simply hasn't had sufficient time to account for the levels, diversity, and sophistication of life that we observe.

Evolutionists try to counter this weakness by talking about huge jumps in the evolutionary process, thus shortening the actual time needed for life to begin. But that only creates another problem for them. We've already seen how statistically improbable evolution is. These types of "miraculous" and random evolutionary jumps required to shorten the time necessary for life to develop only increase the odds against such evolutionary events ever happening.

Reality #5—Momentum. There is no momentum in evolution. The famous drawing of a human emerging from a series of lesser apelike forms implies that evolution gets easier and its odds less improbable as apes become more like men. The drawing reminds me of how a person looks when he is walking up a hill. There is great labor and effort at the steepest parts. But as the person nears the top and the angle decreases, he is able to stand upright as his momentum increases with decreased gravitational resistance. The problem is that there is absolutely no momentum in evolution. There is never a time when evolution gets easier or the gravitational pull against it decreases. Each new transition, mutation, or life-form faces the same impossible odds as its predecessor.

The forces driving evolution have to be stronger than the Second Law of Thermodynamics, which states that things wind down, deteriorate, become less organized, and atrophy when left to themselves. For life—specifically, diverse life—to be produced through evolutionary processes, the power behind it (chance) would have to be greater than the law of decline, which has been proven to be universal. Evolution would have to greatly resemble a snowball that is quite small and slow. As it rolls, it begins to pick up speed. It grows larger, picks up more speed, and grows even larger. Then it hits a bump, a root, or a rock, and it splits and becomes two snowballs. If that process repeats enough times, the small, original snowball could actually grow into a great avalanche. Evolution claims that this is how all life, sophisticated and diverse as it is, came to be—except that in evolution, the snowball is rolling uphill.

Reality #6—The spiritual realm. Science is a discipline that helps us understand the physical world in which we live. It looks at life from a material, measurable, and quantifiable point of view. Humans, however, appear to be more than just physical beings. Every major world religion believes that humans are multidimensional, consisting of body and soul, or body, soul, and spirit, depending on one's terminology. Such distinctly human traits as emotions, love for music, artistic expression, instinctive religious inclinations, and an innate sense of right and wrong are much easier to understand if humans are primarily spiritual beings.

For centuries, scientists and theologians coexisted peacefully. Scientific disciplines spoke to our physical existence, while theology and religion spoke to our spiritual existence. But in the century and a half since Darwin, many scientists have begun to promote science as "the buck stops here" discipline—sort of the Supreme Court of disciplines that study how humans function. The reason? Some scientists believe that humans are not multidimensional. Our existence as an evolved species precludes any sense or need for us to be spiritual beings. Scientists have begun to look at neurology, sociology, and psychology to explain why we have spiritual tendencies. What may look like spiritual behavior— worship, prayer, self-sacrifice—should and can be explained in scientific terms. We pray or worship because our brains evolved with circuitry that included such spiritually inclined behaviors. We sacrifice because our herd instincts tell us to. Thus, science is being set up as the ultimate discipline. If material explanations can be offered for how and why we function the way we do, then we must not be anything more than material beings.

However, many scientific disciplines still reach conclusions or make discoveries that seem to point to a reality or realm that exists beyond the physical level. Recently, a friend of mine who is an agnostic and a retired scientist handed me a video discussing the now-famous Mandelbrot set of fractal shapes. In 1975, Polish mathematician Benoît Mandelbrot coined the term *fractal* to describe a complex geometric shape that, when subdivided, still appears as an exact but smaller replica of the whole. When Mandelbrot placed a fractal shape under a microscope and zoomed in on it, he discovered that it was made up of countless microscopic fractals, each an exact replica of the larger one. When he then magnified one of those smaller fractal forms, he found that they too were made up of countless and infinitely smaller examples of the same fractal shape.

Mandelbrot's experiment might be similar to your placing the entire text of this book, nearly fifty thousand words, under a microscope and then magnifying one specific letter of any word on any page. Suppose you magnified the letter z on this page. As you examined it, you would find that it was made up of millions of tiny little z's, each looking exactly like the original. Then, if you magnified one of those microscopic z's, you would discover that it too was made of up millions of z's, but again infinitely smaller. The difference, however, between what Mandelbrot discovered and my illustration is that Mandelbrot's fractals represent an extremely complicated geometric formula, while my z's are relatively unsophisticated.

Such exact microscopic repetition is astounding to think about, but it's exactly what Mandelbrot uncovered. Mandelbrot has since concluded that the reduction/reproduction capability of fractals is infinite. The strongest microscopes in the world have discovered that the more you magnify a fractal, the more complex fractals you discover. They just go on and on. Mandelbrot has also pointed out examples of fractals in nature—in clouds, mountain ranges, lightning, coastlines, and snowflakes.

Mandelbrot, a very humble but brilliant and highly regarded scientist, openly acknowledged the mystery behind a mathematical formula that could produce such a beautiful and apparently infinite system of design. The reality of fractals seems to imply, at the least, the existence of a realm that we can't see or explain in material terms. And that's what grabbed the attention of my agnostic friend. He admitted that it is difficult to account for the invisible reality implied by the infinite fractal shapes within the traditional boundaries established by science.

The science of quantum physics has for years faced a similar conundrum. Quantum mechanics studies the attributes and relationships of particles on a subatomic level—particles like electrons, protons, and neutrons. While the laws affecting these particles can be observed on microscopic levels, they are not observable on macro or universal levels. Physicists believe that the principles at work in micro quantum physics are also at work at the macro level, but so far such belief exists only in the realm of theory. So while physicists believe the reality of quantum physics exists in the universe, and while they believe they can see the evidence of such physics at work on a microscopic level, they can neither see nor prove that such laws are at work on the universal, macro level. We simply don't have the technology to observe quantum physics at work on such a large scale. In some sense, they have to take such matters on faith. Beyond that, once a physicist opens the door to such specific laws and principles at work on the universal level, he has also opened the door to questions about how those laws came to exist in the first place and what their implications are for life as we know it. That's why almost every thorough treatment of quantum physics includes some discussion of the philosophical and/or religious outcroppings that result from quantum theory.

Once again, science has approached a threshold that it is unable to cross. Where science by definition leaves off, philosophy, religion, and faith begin. There simply aren't adequate physical answers to some of the larger questions science is asking.

In 2 Corinthians 4:18, Paul reminds us of an important eternal truth: "So we fix our eyes not on what is seen, but on what is unseen. For what is seen is temporary, but what is unseen is eternal." Living in a material, physical world, we find it easy to forget about the spiritual realm all around us. When we deal with matters of evolution and creation, it is important that we not overlook the realities of the spiritual world.

Unfortunately, many scientists study the world without giving any thought to spiritual realities. They're only looking for material, measurable, and quantifiable answers to the questions of human origin. Because many of them are not open to a spiritually based answer to the question of how humans came to exist or why there are droughts and earthquakes, they're not looking for one. But science is a physical discipline that is best suited to address material realities. It comes up short when seeking to address invisible or spiritual ones.

Any worldview or philosophy that includes openness to spiritual things has to consider more than just the claims of science. Science is an important discipline that tells us much about the material aspects of our world. But it is not the discipline that trumps all others. In fact, it focuses on a reality—the physical world—that will eventually cease to exist. If anything, in the long run science needs to yield to those disciplines that are better equipped to deal with eternal, spiritual realities.

Why Faith Makes Sense

You have no reason to be intimidated by Darwinian evolution. Please don't let the stream of messages declaring evolution to be a fact distract or discourage you. God is still the only viable explanation for human existence. There are many credible scientists, physicians, biologists, paleontologists, geologists, astronomers, cosmologists, and physicists who take seriously both their science and their faith.

Beyond that, there are issues that lie below the surface of evolution that we need to examine. You might be surprised to know that much of the motivation behind the teaching of macroevolution *isn't* scientific. Darwin's theory of evolution is not the primary opponent to a faith-based perspective. Behind the belief that all life is an evolved accident is a worldview that assumes there is no God, and that worldview is what drives much of the promotion of Darwin's theory. In the next chapter, we'll look at the philosophical viewpoint that presupposes God doesn't exist, contrast it with the faith-based perspective, and consider which is the most intellectually responsible.

6

Who's in Charge Here?

They sit casually around two coffee tables hastily pushed together. Before them is an assortment of snacks and drinks—beer, coffee, bottled water, tea. The group consists of four men—one from India, two Anglo, and one African American—and two females, both Anglo. In the center of the group, his hands gently clasped together in the classic church-steeple style, is the man of Indian descent. He is speaking, and he clearly has the rest of the group's undivided attention.

These conversationalists are part of a growing phenomenon in American culture known as the Socrates Café. Inspired by its namesake's passion for life examination, the Socrates Café consists of adults who meet a few hours a week for the purpose of exchanging ideas. There are no formal rules or regulations in the groups; people just need to bring their ideas and open minds. Groups are springing up in coffeehouses all over the nation. They also have formed in prisons, airport terminals, nursing homes, and even homeless shelters.

Christopher Phillips, the founder of the Socrates Café, has written two books about the movement and travels full-time supporting and starting new groups. He has an interesting goal for the cafés: "The whole idea is not that we find the final answer; it's that we keep thinking about these things."[1] That's actually a pretty savvy business plan. Phillips, like every other great philosopher-turned-entrepreneur, is no dummy. He knows that the secret to good philosophical discussion is to keep the questions coming. The danger of arriving at answers is that one just might put the philosophy business out of business, especially if those answers in any way point to the divine. So finding isn't the point; seeking is.

Phillips and his fellow thinkers have adopted half of the old adage about friendship to never discuss politics or God. In the world of modern philosophical discussion, politics isn't taboo; God is. But Phillips's philosophy invites an interesting question: what's the point of seeking if you're not open to where your search will take you? Why boast in your pursuit of truth if you have a predetermined framework into which truth must fit? Such thinking would be very much like having a map that shows the location of buried treasure but agreeing to follow the map only if it didn't lead to certain places.

Why explore for exploration's sake? Why seek if finding isn't really the point? And why rule out God as a viable answer? Welcome, friends, to the convenient world of humanism.[2]

It's All about Us

The philosophical worldview known as humanism is a broad system of thought that affirms the beauty, dignity, and potential of human beings and basically rejects any notion of

God. Humanists believe that the solutions to the problems humans face can and should be solved by humans, and that the answers to the questions we have about life and our ultimate purpose lie within us, not in some external source. Humanism promotes the concepts of rational thinking and reason but opposes any philosophies that leave open the possibility of the supernatural. And like our curious group of thinkers in the Socrates Café, humanism is all about asking the right questions; finding the actual answers is not the point. Since life is evolving, truth and knowledge are certainly evolving as well. Good thinkers have to be open to the next level or round of truth.

The roots of humanism can be traced as far back as the sixth century BC. Two early Greek thinkers, Thales of Miletus and Xenophanes of Colophon, taught the value of personal introspection (Thales coined the phrase "know thyself") and rejected any divine source for the universe. Not much later, science was promoted as a way of studying the universe without having to acknowledge the supernatural. Agnosticism, if not outright atheism, was the accepted religious worldview of these early "thinkers."

But the fires of humanism began to burn brightest in the early days of the Renaissance. Beginning in Florence, Italy, in the later years of the fourteenth century, humanistic thinking began impacting the religious, social, political, and literary landscape of Europe. Renaissance thinking emphasized the study of Greek and Latin and led to a revived interest in the sciences, philosophy, art, and poetry. Humanist thinkers promoted the disciplines of introspection and self-improvement over biblical disciplines of meditation and prayer. They taught that such qualities as those promoted by Christians—love, generosity, patience, gentleness, and so on—were part and parcel of the human experience and not the result of anything divine. They also taught that biblical concepts such as good and evil were based on an individual's interpretations of both personal and corporate experience, not on any transcendental, objective source.

The ultimate calling card and boasting point for humanism is its claim to own the patent to intelligence and rational thinking. Humanism exalts logic and reason and teaches that they are best expressed in the "respectable" fields of science, literature, and the arts. According to the humanist worldview, it's up to humans to discover truth (if it really exists) and to solve life's mysteries. The answers won't come through any form of divine revelation, but only through the application of logic to observable evidence.

The Anti-God Club

On the surface, humanism sounds like a very friendly and benevolent point of view. Humanists are quick to throw around terms such as *tolerance, peace, democracy, moral excellence,* and *creative thinking.* Here is a sampling of some affirmations taken from the website of the Council for Secular Humanism:

- We believe in an open and pluralistic society and that democracy is the best guarantee of protecting human rights from authoritarian elites and repressive majorities.
- We are concerned with securing justice and fairness in society and with eliminating discrimination and intolerance.
- We believe in supporting the disadvantaged and the handicapped so that they will be able to help themselves.

- We believe in enjoying life here and now and in developing our creative talents to their fullest.
- We believe in the cultivation of moral excellence.
- We believe that scientific discovery and technology can contribute to the betterment of human life.
- We want to protect and enhance the earth, to preserve it for future generations, and to avoid inflicting needless suffering on other species.[3]

Doesn't that sound attractive? Humanists love people, love the planet, want justice for all, and hope you will enjoy your life to the fullest. Who wouldn't agree with those affirmations? Who in their right mind would oppose them?

But don't be fooled by this apparent rose-colored philosophy. At the heart of humanism is a strong anti-God, anti-religion dogma, and most humanists are more than happy to admit it. The name *humanist* is really a pseudonym, because "We believe in humans" is a nicer way of saying, "We don't believe in God."

Consider this mission statement for the Council for Secular Humanism: "The Council for Secular Humanism is North America's leading organization for non-religious people. A not-for-profit educational association, the Council supports a wide range of activities to meet the needs of people who find meaning and value in life without looking to a god."[4] Just so you'll get the full flavor of the anti-God sentiment that lies behind humanism, here are a few more comments:

- [Humanism] is opposed to all varieties of belief that seek supernatural sanction for their values.
- As secular humanists, we are generally skeptical about supernatural claims. We recognize the importance of

religious experience: that experience that redirects and gives meaning to the lives of human beings. We deny, however, that such experiences have anything to do with the supernatural. We are doubtful of traditional views of God and divinity.

- We find that traditional views of the existence of God either are meaningless, have not yet been demonstrated to be true, or are tyrannically exploitative. Secular humanists may be agnostics, atheists, rationalists, or skeptics, but they find insufficient evidence for the claim that some divine purpose exists for the universe. They reject the idea that God has intervened miraculously in history or revealed himself to a chosen few or that he can save or redeem sinners.
- [Humanists] believe that men and women are free and are responsible for their own destinies and that they cannot look toward some transcendent Being for salvation. We reject the divinity of Jesus.
- We deplore efforts to denigrate human intelligence, to seek to explain the world in supernatural terms, and to look outside nature for salvation.[5]

I find those comments to be rather interesting. It seems that humanists' claims to being open-minded have their limits. At least they're honest about their boundaries: they're willing to seek truth, just as long as that truth doesn't lead them in the direction of God.

What's the Big Deal?

You might be saying, "So what? So there's a group of people out there who have organized themselves around their mutual disbelief in God. Is that bad? That's certainly their right. What's the big deal?" Great question. Here's my answer: the big deal is that in the last one hundred years, humanism has become the operational worldview for some of our nation's most powerful institutions, including government, the media, and higher education. And humanism, not scientific evidence, is the driving force behind the teaching and aggressive promotion of macroevolution as fact.

At the core of humanism is the belief that man is the highest reality. It asserts that humans are the highest form of life and that no other forms of life (physical or spiritual) exist beyond us. Therefore, there has to be a mechanical, material explanation for how we got here. Since humanists begin with the presupposition that God is out of the equation, they have to find a way to account for life that appears scientifically viable and doesn't allow or need any input from the divine.

Enter Darwinism. With the advent and mass acceptance of macroevolutionary theory, humanists found their material explanation for life's existence. Beyond that, Darwinism gave humanist thinkers the perfect bully pulpit from which to promote their anti-God sentiment. And that they have done. It is no longer in vogue in mainstream science to consider that God might have had something to do with how we got here. Rather, those scientists who still entertain the notion of the divine are often branded as being weak-minded or not true scientists at all.

And therein lies the point you need to grasp as you weigh the validity of your faith: evolutionists' claims that there is no God are not based on any evidence that disproves God; they are based on a worldview that requires a world without God. Behind the rhetoric of the atheists' bestsellers and media reports of the latest scientific discoveries that render God unnecessary is a philosophical viewpoint that assumes God doesn't exist.

Humanists have commandeered science and reason as their one-two punch in the battle over what's real and what isn't, and they're quick to label any viewpoint that still holds to the existence of God as "irrational," "unscientific," and "lacking reason."

Consider the following humanist beliefs:

- We consider the universe to be a dynamic scene of natural forces that are most effectively understood by scientific inquiry.

- We view with concern the current attack by nonsecularists on reason and science. We are committed to the use of the rational methods of inquiry, logic, and evidence in developing knowledge and testing claims to truth.

- Today the theory of evolution is again under heavy attack by religious fundamentalists. There may be some significant differences among scientists concerning the mechanics of evolution; yet the evolution of the species is supported so strongly by the weight of evidence that it is difficult to reject it. Accordingly, we deplore the efforts by fundamentalists (especially in the United States) to invade the science classrooms, requiring that creationist theory be taught to students and requiring that it be included in biology textbooks. This is a serious threat both to academic freedom and to the integrity of the educational process. . . . But it is a sham to mask an article of religious faith as a scientific truth and to inflict that doctrine on the scientific curriculum. If successful, creationists may seriously undermine the credibility of science itself.[6]

Obviously, humanists understand that the stakes are high. They're right. But does drawing spiritual conclusions from scientific discoveries really threaten the integrity of the scientific process? Or are humanists just sounding the alarm as the battle heats up around them? And what, really, is the battle about?

More Than Just an Identity Crisis

At the center of this discussion is the collision of two opposing and mutually exclusive worldviews. One (humanism) rejects the notion of God, while the other (theism) embraces it. As you can imagine, the views of reality from the human-centered world and the God-centered world are quite different. But beyond that, the human-centered world can't account for much of how humans live and function. Their bottom-line belief in humans as the ultimate reality has major holes in it. Let's consider a few of them.

A human-centered worldview can't account for how we got here. Macroevolution is offered as the best explanation for the mechanics of *how* life exists, but it doesn't explain *why* life exists in the first place. As we saw in the previous chapters, the question of First Cause can't be readily answered in an evolved world. Thus, humanists are faced with the difficult task of trying to explain our existence without being able to point to a source outside ourselves. The question goes well beyond the classic quandary, "Which came first, the chicken or the egg?" It must instead answer the question, "Whichever came first, how did it get here?"—without being able to consider the variables of a rancher, a market, or a chicken coop.

In a God-centered worldview, no such quandary exists. We are here because God created us and placed us here. Our world appears to be miraculously fine-tuned to support our existence because it is. Humanists will counter by asking, "Who made God?" But such a question is a reflection of their limited point of view. In a reality that allows for a divine being, the possibility of his self-existence isn't unreasonable.

A human-centered worldview has a difficult time explaining our search for meaning and purpose. If you think about it, the fact that humanism promotes philosophy and the search for truth is a bit ironic. Humanism claims that we evolved from dust and that there is no design or purpose to our existence. We are the result of the forces of blind chance at work. Why, then, should we seek meaning? Why should we seek answers to life's most pressing questions when none exist?

In a God-centered worldview, we have been created to have a relationship with our Creator. We exist to love and glorify God. We search for meaning and purpose in our lives because God has wired us for that search. It's part of our spiritual DNA.

Philosopher Blaise Pascal argued that we search for meaning because we have a "God-shaped void" within us. We look for something to complete us. What we are looking for is God. The apostle Paul shared a similar thought: "God did this so that men would seek him and perhaps reach out for him and find him, though he is not far from each one of us. 'For in him we live and move and have our being'" (Acts 17:27–28).

A human-centered worldview can't explain why we care for the weak and seek to improve life for all. Earlier in the chapter, I showed you several noble-sounding affirmations of humanism. Two of them read:

- We are concerned with securing justice and fairness in society and with eliminating discrimination and intolerance.

- We believe in supporting the disadvantaged and the handicapped so that they will be able to help themselves.

But those two statements are inconsistent with the overall philosophy that accompanies humanism's flagship doctrine of macroevolution. In an evolved world, the weak in society shouldn't be protected. Darwin's theories of natural selection and survival of the fittest state that in order for life to both survive and evolve, the weaker elements of a species have to be selected out. Evolution thrives on the cutthroat, uncaring removal and extinction of those life-forms that can't survive on their own.

Isn't it hypocritical, then, for humanists to talk about supporting the weak in culture? Since we're evolved, why should we make allowances for those with special needs? Why offer protection for minorities? Why provide the less fortunate in society with social benefits? In an evolved world, society should be allowed to eliminate its weaker members. In an evolved culture, what Hitler did wasn't wrong. He was just a powerful, well-organized example of human natural selection at work. There is no difference between the extinction of animals and the extinction of certain types of humans. Both reflect natural laws at work.

Humanists love to talk about the value of every human, even weak ones. But there is no personal value in an evolved world. We are mere accidental products of our environment. We can't boast in our value, because we have none.

In a God-centered worldview, every human is of infinite value to God. Our value isn't based on our appearance, what contribution we make to society, our education, our income level, or our skin color. We are made in the image of a holy

God, and that alone is sufficient to make us valuable—both to God and to each other.

A human-centered worldview says that evil is a figment of our imaginations. In a human-centered society, evil doesn't really exist. Good and bad behavior and our innate sense of right and wrong are evidence of our brains' functioning, or malfunctioning, and not evidence of some super-sinister force at work.[7] The notion that something is evil requires that there be something opposite of evil. For evil to be real and definable, there has to be a standard that is not evil—good—so that evil can be recognized. Humanism can't embrace the concepts of ultimate good or evil, because those concepts imply an ultimate standard by which they can be measured. Rather, humanism relies on our collective human judgment—what seems good or what seems bad to the whole—for establishing our moral boundaries.

In a God-centered worldview, the Bible offers clear and uncompromising explanations for what we call evil: Satan and sin. In biblical thinking, all evil, sickness, hatred, and even death in the world can be explained by the sin disease that affects all humans. Satan is considered to be real, powerful, and destructive. We aren't given a pass for our bad behavior because of Satan's existence, but we do need to be rescued from Satan's clutches.

The problem with humanism's interpretation of good and evil is that they become a moving target, subject to the direction of the prevailing cultural winds. How long will it be before the kind of brutality applauded in the Roman coliseum is deemed acceptable by the whole? In a God-centered world, good and bad isn't left up to us to determine. The lines are clearly drawn for us by our holy Creator. What is left to our discretion, however, is whether or not we will adhere to the

God-given laws that will help promote peace and civility in our culture.

A human-centered worldview leads to the conclusion that through evolution we become the very thing humanism claims does not exist. This may be the most ironic point of all. Humanists have to grant that we already live at a much higher level of sophistication than our animal cousins. Otherwise, they have no valid explanations for such highly developed human concepts as beauty, art, music, love, and, of course, morality. If humans are evolved, then something very substantial happened in the jump between apes and us, for humans are far superior to apes.

One can only wonder what type of dramatic jumps still lie ahead for us in the evolutionary process. Whatever they may be, there will no doubt come a point when we will cease to be "human" and become something else altogether, something far and dynamically superior to humans. This new, evolved species will seem as great and superior to humans as humans do to apes. Wouldn't that new, evolved, superior species be the same as something we might call *divine*? How much do humans have to evolve before they cross the line from being mortal to being immortal? In the worldview of humanism, the day will surely come when evolution finds a way to overcome death, when the reigning species on earth will indeed be just that—reigning. But wouldn't that new species be godlike, at least as far as we understand godlikeness? Do you see the irony in that? The very thing that humanism argues against is the precise thing that evolution ends up producing—god. The writers of *Time* magazine put it this way: "After millions of years, evolution by natural selection, operating blindly and randomly, has produced a creature capable of overturning evolution itself. Where we go from here is now up to us."[8]

In a God-centered worldview, the lines between divinity and humanity are clearly drawn. In Psalm 8 David declared, "O LORD, our Lord, how majestic is your name in all the earth! You have set your glory above the heavens. . . . When I consider your heavens, the work of your fingers, the moon and the stars, which you have set in place, what is man that you are mindful of him, the son of man that you care for him?" (vv. 1, 3–4). In a biblical framework, humans are part of a glorious creation that is completely dependent upon its creator. We exist by God and for God (see Col. 1:16). We are not god, and we will not evolve into god. The splendor of being human is found in glorifying and honoring the God who made us, not in exalting ourselves over him.

The Biggest Problem with Humanism

There is one additional point we need to consider when weighing the validity of the human-centered reality. It is the greatest weakness humanism faces. In a word, it's *humans*. Humanism bets the proverbial farm on the ability of humankind to work the kinks out of our system and improve ourselves. It assumes and hopes that we won't always be selfish, prejudiced, hateful, and murderous. It believes that we will someday crack the code on our weaknesses and somehow get better.

Because humanism rejects the concept of sin and believes that there is nothing wrong with humans that a little more reason and learning can't fix, its hopes lie in the goodness of people—specifically, future people. It's banking on a future generation of humans to somehow overcome the gravitational pull of selfishness, greed, lust, and pride and to rise to some human-produced brand of nirvana.

Interestingly, Jesus, who from the humanists' standpoint is arguably one of the greatest humans in history, didn't place a lot of stock in our capacity to fix ourselves. His disciple John wrote, "But Jesus would not entrust himself to them, for he knew all men. He did not need man's testimony about man, for he knew what was in a man" (John 2:24–25). Whatever Jesus saw in humans, it didn't produce any hope in him for the future of humanity. Rather, Jesus's life mission was to point us to a means of salvation that lay beyond ourselves.

And that is the heart of the difference between the human-centered and God-centered worlds. Both agree that we need saving; they just disagree on our best hope for salvation.

Starry, Starry Night

Once in the spring of 2001, my daughter Emily and I rose at 3:00 a.m. to watch a NASA space shuttle make reentry over our city. We drove a few blocks from our house to a hill with a spectacular view toward the west, since the shuttle would be coming in over the West Coast. While we waited for the shuttle's appearance, Emily and I stood transfixed by all the brilliant stars. Even though they were somewhat dulled by the city's glow, they were still spectacular.

Our fixation with the stars was quickly interrupted by the sudden appearance of a streaking yellow light on the western horizon that seemed to be climbing straight up. It was the shuttle, and it was an amazing sight. Silently and effortlessly, this machine cut a path across the morning sky, leaving a huge vapor trail glowing in its wake. Even though the shuttle was passing eighty miles north of our city, it seemed as if it was right above us. We watched for about three minutes until the shuttle faded from view, at that point only a few minutes away from touchdown in Florida. My daughter and I got back into our car and drove quickly back to our house. As we were walking in the front door, we heard the loud sonic boom from the shuttle. It had taken those few minutes for the sound to reach us. Tired though we were, we were impressed.

No one watching the shuttle's spectacular reentry that morning would ever believe that such a magnificent machine was the result of some accident or even a series of accidents. We all know better. The scientists and engineers who designed, built, tested, and operated the shuttle would be more than offended if anyone were to seriously suggest such a thing. No thinking person would. Things with such high levels of sophistication don't *just happen*. The technology and learning required to send men and women to space and back is truly astonishing.

After the glow of the shuttle's vapor trail faded away, there before our awe-filled eyes was a spectacular sky filled with more stars than we could ever count. Stretched out before us was a massive universe, the ends of which we still can't find. Glowing from hundreds of millions of light-years away were balls of fire more powerful and long lasting than anything humans can ever even dream of creating. And yet we're supposed to believe that such an awesome, powerful display of cosmic grandeur is accidental and random. We're supposed to believe that the eyes we use to take in the sky's majesty and the brain we use to process the visual information we receive are also random. We're supposed to believe that while a space shuttle is clearly the work of intelligent sources, the massive universe, which the shuttle is designed to explore, isn't. And we're supposed to believe that there is no such thing as a holy, creating, and life-giving God behind everything. In other words, we should believe in what humans can do but not in what God did. Sometimes the arrogance of the human mind is astounding. "Who are you that you fear mortal men, the sons of men, who are but grass, that you forget the LORD your Maker, who stretched out the heavens and laid the foundations of the earth?" (Isa. 51:12–13).

Why Faith Makes Sense

The Bible makes some very reasonable claims: We are created by a holy God. We exist because of him, and we exist for him. I submit to you that belief in the creative work of a holy God is more rational and intellectually plausible than the randomness of life proposed by humanism. It isn't irrational to see evidence of an all-powerful God in the created world. Neither is it irrational to believe that such a creating God is the hope of the world. In part 3, we'll see just how reasonable and plausible our faith really is.

THINK ON THESE THINGS

One of the strong lines of argument for the truth of the resurrection is the astonishing transformation of the disciples from the demoralized, defeated men of Good Friday to the confident proclaimers of the Lordship of Christ at Pentecost and beyond, even to the point of martyrdom. Something happened to bring that about. I believe it was the resurrection and that if Jesus had not been raised it is probable that we would never have heard of him.

John Polkinghorne, past president and Fellow
from Queen's College, Cambridge

7

A Thinking Person's Guide to Faith

I met Kat several summers ago when my family and I spent a week at an Alaskan fishing camp. A twentysomething who had escaped from the pressures of city life by spending her summer working in the beauty of our northernmost state, Kat was an avowed agnostic. She had grown up in church, had eventually found the whole thing to be irrelevant, and had written off both the church and Christianity.

I took an immediate interest in Kat. I prayed for her and spent many hours talking with her about matters of faith. I remember asking Kat question after question: Was life accidental? Where did we come from? Had she grown up in church? Did her parents believe? Had she ever read the Bible?

I was amazed at what I learned. This young, bright agnostic had chosen her faith—or lack thereof—by default. She hadn't really thought about the Bible or matters of faith.

I'll never forget, at one point in our discussion, Kat's comment: "You're asking me to turn on my brain." Exactly. Most people, when they really think about it, find faith to be quite tenable. Those who don't are frequently guilty of turning off their brains. Let's look at how Christians are actually called to use their minds.

The Bible and Your Brain

The Bible is the sourcebook of the Christian church. It is the sole authoritative work for those who follow Jesus Christ. As such, it's the book that hundreds of millions read for inspiration, guidance, and instruction. But for such an ancient document, the Bible has unmatched levels of internal and external evidence for its accuracy and authority. If you're looking for a religious guidebook that doesn't ask you to make a blind leap in the dark to accept its word, then look no further than the Bible. Here are just a few of the reasons that you can trust the veracity of the Bible.[1]

Historical Documentation

As an ancient literary work, the New Testament is the best-documented piece of literature in history. There are more ancient and accurate copies of the New Testament (over five thousand) than the works of Plato or Aristotle (each with fewer than five ancient copies). No other ancient work boasts anywhere near the number of copies as the New Testament. With the discovery of the Dead Sea Scrolls in 1948, the case for the veracity of the Old Testament (a much older document) gained significant ground as well. In short, most who refute Christianity on the grounds that the Bible is inaccurate do so on the basis of false information. If someone could have proven Christ a fraud based on the Bible's textual shortcomings, he or she would have already done so.

Authorship

The sixty-six books of the Bible were written over a period of 1,600 to 1,700 years. The oldest book, probably Job, was written at least 1,600 years before Christ. The most recent, Revelation, was written in AD 90. We know that forty writers and/or editors produced the various books of the Bible, working from three different continents in three different languages. And yet, even with its high number of contributors and their diverse backgrounds, the Bible has an uncanny degree of unity and seamlessness to its message and story.

Compilation

The Bible didn't become the Bible overnight. In fact, it took over three hundred years for the sixty-six books to finally be recognized as the authoritative sourcebook of the Christian church. In the case of the New Testament, individual books were written and circulated to various churches in the first century AD. They slowly came to be viewed as authoritative based on the known credentials of the author and their content. Later, the authoritative letters began to be collected and circulated together in groups. It wasn't until AD 397, at a gathering of church leaders at Carthage in North Africa, that twenty-seven books were officially affirmed as the New Testament canon of the church.[2] Compared to the Qur'an, the Bhagavad Gita, the book of Mormon, and other religious sourcebooks, the compilation and organization of the Bible included an amazingly high number of people. God used thousands of individuals over hundreds of years to put together what we now know as the Holy Scriptures.

Message

I frequently get asked how I can believe in the relevance of a book that is as old as the Bible. How can it possibly have anything to say about today's sophisticated world? I typically respond by asking the person if he or she has actually read the Bible. In my experience, it's anything but irrelevant. In fact, it's painfully relevant. How can a book that openly discusses murder, jealousy, racism, divorce, fear, financial management, slavery, the oppression of women in society, conflict resolution, prayer, the value of humanity, heaven, hell, death, suffering, leadership, pride, human origins, ethics and morality, capital punishment, child rearing, marriage, sexuality, evil, physical health and well-being, governmental authority and civic responsibility, taxes, the spiritual realm, witchcraft, demonic worship, astrology, alcohol use, and the Palestinian/Israeli conflict be deemed irrelevant? Add in the Bible's generous offerings of wisdom and instruction on life's most pressing issues, and you end up with a timeless treasure that speaks to the ages.

Durability

The Bible is, without exception, the most attacked and maligned book in history. Every generation since Christ has had its outspoken critics of the Bible and its message. Today is no exception. Some scholars today have banded together to try to show that much of the New Testament is erroneous and that Jesus neither said nor did much of what is credited to him. It is, however, the height of arrogance to assume that those of us who are living two thousand years after an event can know what really happened better than those who observed or experienced it.

François Marie Arouet (1694–1778) was a French philosopher and atheist who wrote under the pen name Voltaire.

He predicted that Christianity would be an extinct religion within one hundred years of his life. Fifty years after his death, in 1828, his house was purchased by the Geneva Bible Society, a well-known mission organization that translates and distributes the Bible. The society set up a printing press in the atheist's former home, produced thousands of copies of Scripture, and distributed them around the world.

Recognizing the Bible as a helpful and reliable tool for your spiritual pursuits isn't a foolish venture. It is without question the best-documented and most historically and archaeologically substantiated religious text in the world.[3] Beyond that, its evidences of divine inspiration—its ability to produce radical life change and lead people from all walks of life to faith in Christ—are undeniable. Those who become students of the Bible won't be inhibiting their minds but rather will be stimulating them.

Put On Your Thinking Cap

The Bible speaks frequently to the concepts of wisdom, knowledge, and learning. In fact, the Bible is replete with calls for its readers to think, and it associates good thinking with a proper perspective on God. Consider the following:

> But if not, then listen to me;
> be silent, and I will teach you wisdom.
>
> Job 33:33

> Who endowed the heart with wisdom
> or gave understanding to the mind?
>
> Job 38:36

I will instruct you and teach you in the way you should go;
   I will counsel you and watch over you.

                                             Psalm 32:8

Instruct a wise man and he will be wiser still;
   teach a righteous man and he will add to his learning.

                                             Proverbs 9:9

Buy the truth and do not sell it;
   get wisdom, discipline and understanding.

                                             Proverbs 23:23

All this I saw, as I applied my mind to everything done under
the sun.

                                             Ecclesiastes 8:9

"Come now, let us reason together,"
   says the LORD.

                                             Isaiah 1:18

No one stops to think,
   no one has the knowledge or understanding to say,
   "Half of it I used for fuel;
   I even baked bread over its coals,
   I roasted meat and I ate.
   Shall I make a detestable thing from what is left?
   Shall I bow down to a block of wood?"

                                             Isaiah 44:19

Therefore everyone who hears these words of mine and puts
them into practice is like a wise man who built his house
on the rock.

                                             Matthew 7:24

Take my yoke upon you and learn from me, for I am gentle and humble in heart, and you will find rest for your souls.

Matthew 11:29

What do you think about the Christ? Whose son is he?

Matthew 22:42

For although they knew God, they neither glorified him as God nor gave thanks to him, but their thinking became futile and their foolish hearts were darkened.

Romans 1:21

Finally, brothers, whatever is true, whatever is noble, whatever is right, whatever is pure, whatever is lovely, whatever is admirable—if anything is excellent or praiseworthy—think about such things.

Philippians 4:8

We have much to say about this, but it is hard to explain because you are slow to learn.

Hebrews 5:11

Dear friends, this is now my second letter to you. I have written both of them as reminders to stimulate you to wholesome thinking.

2 Peter 3:1

I could go on, but you get the point. Anyone who says that the Bible is a book for dummies has never seriously read it. Lofty topics such as knowledge, learning, wisdom, discernment, contemplation, meditation, divine revelation, study and discipline, personal development, intellectual training, and philosophy run cover to cover. In fact, the Bible itself is no light read. When was the last time you heard of someone who quit reading the Bible because it was too *easy* to understand?

The Bible is not a book of watered-down philosophy and simplistic faith. It deals with life's most pressing and difficult questions. It offers a consistent call for men and women who are pursuing ultimate truth to use their minds in the process. For the biblical writers, there was no separating the pursuit of God from thinking. The former simply could not be discovered without the latter.

Ambushed by Faith

C. S. Lewis was one of the greatest Christian thinkers in the twentieth century. However, that was not always the case. For many decades he was a hardened atheist whose disbelief was fostered in the world of academic pride that he had embraced.

In his book *Surprised by Joy*, Lewis reflected on the atheism that he had practiced for so many years: "The accepted position seemed to be that religions were normally a mere farrago of nonsense. . . . But the impression I got was that religion in general, though utterly false, was a natural growth, a kind of endemic nonsense into which humanity tended to blunder."[4]

But Lewis's atheism didn't stick. It seemed the philosophy of intellectual isolation that he embraced continually left him wanting answers. In 1929, after a long period of struggling with the rationale of belief, Lewis finally conceded defeat and officially embraced theism (belief in God). About his "conversion" he wrote, "In the Trinity Term of 1929 I gave in, and admitted that God was God, and knelt and prayed; perhaps, that night, the most dejected and reluctant convert in all of England."[5] Lewis, it seems, had done his best to resist the gnawing feeling within him that God was indeed real. But resist he couldn't, and his intellectual atheism was changed into intellectual theism.

Two years later, partly due to the influence of J. R. R. Tolkien and Hugo Dyson, Lewis embraced Christianity. He spent the next thirty years as one of the world's leading apologists for the Christian faith. His classic work *Mere Christianity* remains a primary starting point for many thinking agnostics and atheists who want to at least consider the validity of Christianity, and for many Christians who want to better understand the connection between faith and reason.

So the thinker became a believer. But does that mean he stopped thinking? Quite the contrary. Lewis later came to the conclusion that even his ability to reason came from God. He wrote: "There is a difficulty in disagreeing with God. He is the source from which all your reasoning power comes: You could not be right and he wrong any more than a stream can rise higher than its own source. When you are arguing against him you are arguing against the very power that makes you able to argue at all: It is like cutting off the branch you are sitting on."[6]

The Search for True Wisdom

I'd like to introduce you to another great thinker: King Solomon. Solomon ruled over the united monarchy of Israel for the last forty years of the eleventh century BC. The son of the fiery and passionate king David, Solomon was an even more effective leader than his father. He led Israel at the height of her military, economic, and political power. There has never been a time when Israel was blessed with more peace and national prosperity than under Solomon's reign. His reign truly represented the glory days of Israel.

Solomon was famous for many things, but none more so than for his wisdom. He was legendary for the levels of understanding and insight he showed in the practical matters of life. Solomon was a student all his life. He diligently pursued the highest levels of knowledge available to him. The books of Proverbs and Ecclesiastes are two of the most practical and philosophical, respectively, in the Old Testament. Both are thought to have been either written or edited by Solomon. Proverbs is a collection of sayings about wisdom, learning, and pragmatic lessons for life. Some were no doubt original to Solomon, but many were truths he had learned in his pursuit of knowledge. Ecclesiastes is a deeply philosophical and reflective work. In it Solomon records his own efforts and struggles to discern the ultimate meaning of life.

As king of the greatest nation on earth, Solomon was denied no pleasure. Wealth, fame, prestige, power, sex, servants, and palaces—if pleasure could make a guy happy, then Solomon should have been the happiest man on earth. But he wasn't. He actually found that all his stuff only made him hungrier for ultimate meaning. So he began a pursuit of truth. He gave the better years of his adulthood to solving the mystery (there's that word again) of the meaning of life. Here's his own description of his search: "So I turned my mind to understand, to investigate and to search out wisdom and the scheme of things and to understand the stupidity of wickedness and the madness of folly" (Eccles. 7:25).

Solomon figured that there was more to life than what he could see and certainly more than what he had. So off he went on his journey for ultimate meaning. He recorded in Proverbs one of the conclusions of his search: "The fear of the LORD is the beginning of wisdom, and knowledge of the Holy One is understanding" (Prov. 9:10). Isn't that interesting? After gratifying his flesh and feeding his desires, and after searching far and wide for real meaning, Solomon concluded that true knowledge and understanding began with a proper fear of God. (Remember that when Solomon spoke of fear, he didn't mean fear as in the *terror* kind, he meant fear as in the *awe and respect* kind.) Solomon determined that if people were serious about unlocking life's secrets, and if they really wanted to think profound thoughts and know ultimate truths, then they had better begin their efforts by acknowledging God. He concluded that God is the keeper of all true knowledge. Solomon, a man heralded as the wisest of his day, realized that if he really wanted to be smart, then he needed to go to the only source who could teach him things that he could not learn anywhere else—God.

Such thinking sounds a bit archaic today. We live in a society that completely exalts the mind. Conventional wisdom says that given enough time, the human mind can pretty much solve any problem set before it. As we have seen, evolutionary theory says that humanity is in the process, albeit a slow one, of evolving to an even greater and higher plane of existence. Problems and issues we face today may be insignificant, if not nonexistent, after a few more human evolutionary cycles. In other words, our minds are sufficient. The mantra of today's leading thinkers is not that we need more humility but that we need more learning. As we saw in chapter 6, we don't need faith in God, we just need to think and grow our way into higher levels of intellectual sophistication. The implication is that the more we know, the better our overall quality of life as humans will be.

Perhaps this is why those who strongly support one side or the other of the mind vs. faith issue often fail to meet anywhere near the middle. Those in the faith camp see the others as arrogant, self-impressed, and faithless. Those on the side of intellect see "believers" as backward, naive, and uninformed. The irony is that the Bible allows for no such dichotomy. God simply did not create a system that requires a person to segregate any part of the body, mind, and soul in order to know him.

I Think, Therefore I Believe

The biblical call to think rings loud and clear in the New Testament. The apostle Paul frequently argued for the validity of Jesus Christ from a predominantly intellectual standpoint. In the early years of his ministry, he was fond of setting up shop right in the middle of a room of stoics and skeptics and debating with them about the message of Christ. Luke, the physician-turned-biblical writer, often used a form of the word *reason* to describe Paul's methods. For instance, in Acts 18:4, Luke wrote, "Every Sabbath he reasoned in the synagogue, trying to persuade Jews and Greeks." The word translated "reasoned" is the Greek word *dialegomai*, and you may recognize its resemblance to the English word *dialogue*. And that's precisely what it means: "to reason," "to thoroughly discuss," "to talk through," "to analyze," "to debate," or "to dispute." When Paul decided to engage such mental heavyweights as the Athenians in a discussion of the Christian faith, he didn't ask them to set aside their mental processes. Rather, he addressed them from the standpoint where they were most confident: that of reason. But Paul wasn't making some big sacrifice to do so, and neither was he putting himself at a disadvantage. If anything, he was posturing himself to win the debate and to persuade his fellow thinkers.

Paul believed to his core that if the Christian message was anything, it was reasonable. He believed that all truth is ultimately God's truth and that any genuine search for truth would inevitably lead to God. Paul wasn't the least bit afraid of the Athenians' reputation for profound philosophizing. Actually, he felt better set up to speak their language because they were thinkers. Isn't it interesting to note that our faith's greatest apologist was known for his reasoning capabilities?

So was Paul an exception? Was he some Christian anomaly who somehow managed to combine faith and reason without becoming too consumed by either? Or was Paul the norm? Was he an example of how a thinking person can come to terms with God by using his or her mind? And if so, could that give you hope that when you jump into a relationship with God, you'll be encouraged—even expected—to use your brain?

Knowing God

In Paul's writings, we see even more of his belief in the marriage of reason and faith. He seemed almost obsessed with the connection between profound knowledge and a profound faith. In Paul's mind, as learning and understanding increased, so did belief. He saw a clear proportional relationship between *knowledge of* and *faith in* God. The more a person knew of God, the more likely he or she was to believe in him. Ignorance of God produced unbelief; knowledge of God increased faith. For Paul, that meant he couldn't divorce his heart from his head. He called followers of Christ all over the ancient world to put their minds fully into the task of seeking God. Here are just a few examples:

- Paul challenged the believers in Ephesus to function in their spiritual gifts so that they might "reach unity in the faith and in the knowledge of the Son of God and become mature, attaining to the whole measure of the fullness of Christ" (Eph. 4:13). Paul believed that a church unified in its belief in and knowledge of Jesus would lead to corporate, spiritual maturity in the body.

- Paul prayed that the believers in Philippi might grow in their "knowledge and depth of insight" so they might discern God's best for them and live blameless lives (Phil. 1:9–10).

- Paul asked God to fill the Christians in Colossae with the "knowledge of his will through all spiritual wisdom and understanding" (Col. 1:9).

- Paul told his young apprentice, Timothy, that God wanted all men "to come to a knowledge of the truth" of Jesus (1 Tim. 2:4).

- Paul told his friend and fellow pastor, Titus, who ministered on the Greek isle of Crete, that it was "knowledge of the truth that leads to godliness" in a person (Titus 1:1).

- Paul prayed that his friends in Ephesus might have "the Spirit of wisdom and revelation" so that they might know God better (Eph. 1:17).

- Twenty-five times in his letters, Paul mentioned wisdom, and another nineteen times he talked about being wise.

- Over twenty-five times in his letters, Paul discussed the importance of the mind in knowing and following God.

- In his final letter before his execution, Paul urged Timothy to hurry to his side and to bring the "parchments" with him (2 Tim. 4:13). Even late in life, with death hanging over his head, Paul wanted to study.

It's difficult to see Paul as one who advocated a superficial faith. He seemed to believe strongly that any serious pursuer of the Christian God had better be ready to engage his mind in the process.

Put Your Mind into It

Perhaps the best testimony to the mental requirements of the Christian faith came from its founder, Jesus Christ. Jesus invited men and women to a faith that by nature encompassed their brains. Jesus claimed to speak for the God of all creation, and creation certainly included the human mind. Had Jesus offered a faith system that did not engage the human mind, he would have been presenting a system that was inconsistent with the God he claimed to know.

In a crescendo passage in the New Testament, Jesus was asked about the Hebrew law of Moses. What, in Jesus's opinion, was the most important part? Jesus didn't even hesitate in his answer: "Love the Lord your God with all your heart and with all your soul and with all your mind" (Matt. 22:37). In this response, Jesus quoted from a very well-known passage in Deuteronomy. Centuries before, God had made his expectations for his followers quite clear through Moses. He wanted a nation of followers who were fully engaged with him, and that included being mentally engaged. Basically, Jesus was saying that one-third of the great commandment was to love God with our minds.

So how do we do that? How do we love God mentally? Wouldn't it mean using our minds to their fullest potential? Wouldn't it also mean disciplining ourselves to think high and profound thoughts? Shouldn't we choose to be stewards of the incredible tool of our minds that God has given us?

To love God with all our minds is to throw every bit of mental energy we have into pursuing him. It means not wasting the potential of our minds and not filling our minds with junk. It means requiring our minds to think, meditate, contemplate, and be stretched so that God might use them for his glory. To love God with all our minds means to submit our minds to him. And that, according to both testaments of the Bible, is where true wisdom and knowledge begin.

Jesus Christ never promoted mental lethargy. Christianity, a faith that was birthed out of the instruction-oriented world of Judaism, cannot function or be propagated without learning. Jesus taught that not using our minds was a complete mismanagement of one of the greatest assets that God has given us—our brains. Jesus, like the apostle Paul, who was one of his greatest proponents, believed that it was impossible to succeed in Christianity without using your mind. Implicit in the call to follow Christ is the call to think.

Why Faith Makes Sense

So how do you respond to Jesus's and Paul's teachings? Christianity is a faith that invites you to think profound thoughts and to have your mind enlightened by God. If you are a follower of Jesus Christ, then you are commanded to submit your mind to him. It's not yours to manage (or mismanage). Jesus fully expects you to learn how to think on a spiritual plane so that you can both know him better and communicate about him more effectively. Anything less is disobedience.

If you're not yet a Christ-follower, consider this invitation from God, spoken through Isaiah the prophet some seven hundred years before Christ: "'Come now, let us *reason* together,' says the LORD. 'Though your sins are like scarlet, they shall be as white as snow; though they are red as crimson, they shall be like wool'" (Isa. 1:18, emphasis added).

And what about our great thinker, King Solomon? What was the result of his search? Let's let him tell us himself: "Now all has been heard; here is the conclusion of the matter: Fear God and keep his commandments, for this is the whole duty of man. For God will bring every deed into judgment, including every hidden thing, whether it is good or evil" (Eccles. 12:13–14).

8

God's Self-Portrait

Todd is seventeen, lanky, and going into his senior year in high school. He is a typical teen in many ways—he likes girls, makes decent grades, and loves playing basketball and hanging out with his friends. His parents divorced when he was young; as a result, Todd quit going to church and lost his sources for any helpful spiritual input.

Recently, when Todd came within an inch of being killed in a car wreck, he decided it was time to get some answers about God. His dad asked me to stop by after work one day to see if I could help Todd with his spiritual pursuits. I was glad to oblige.

Todd told me that he would lie awake at night praying, but he wasn't sure if God ever heard him. He was concerned because he had never heard God talk back to him. Beyond that, Todd had a myriad of typical questions: What is God like? Is he good? Did he really create everything? Why does he let so many bad things happen? Is heaven real? If so, how

125

do you get there? And, perhaps most importantly, how could he really know God?

I sat down with Todd at his dining room table and talked casually with him about faith. I affirmed him for his openness, for his humility, and for his questions. I encouraged him to keep seeking and told him it's very difficult to mess up a search for God. The great thing about looking for God is that he wants to be found. If you seek him with integrity and authenticity, you'll find him.

Then I gave Todd an assignment. I told him to explore Jesus Christ. I told Todd that if he really wanted to find God, he had to get to know Jesus. I left Todd with his Bible and his promise to start reading the Gospels.

Why did I do that? Why did I encourage a spiritually inquisitive teenager who was looking for God to pursue Jesus Christ? Todd hadn't asked about Jesus, he had asked about God. So why tell him to look into Jesus? Because in the Christian faith, the living proof of God's existence, character, and nature is Jesus. Other religions offer all sorts of ways and strategies to get to God. Not Christianity. The path it offers to God is notoriously narrow, and its teaching couldn't be more direct: seeking people like Todd need to pursue a relationship with Jesus Christ, because he is the best, clearest, most definitive picture of God that we will ever receive.

Closing the Gap

There is indeed a large gap that exists between belief in God and belief in Jesus. While there are many who will acknowledge the obvious existence of some divine, creative power, they're still a long way from embracing Jesus as God's Son. In this chapter and the next, we will address the unique role that Jesus plays in history as the only way to God, some common objections to faith in Jesus, the scandalous question of the exclusivity of the Christian faith, and why it makes good rational sense to believe in Jesus.

At the beginning of this book, we talked about mystery—specifically, the mystery of God. We learned that God, by nature, is shrouded in mystery. If we are to know him, then he has to lead us to himself. Any efforts of our own to discover him will fall short. His infinite nature will simply elude us.

Enter revelation. We learned that revelation is the process by which God makes himself known, and it almost always includes contact with the human mind. There are two levels of revelation, and we've already looked at the first one—natural revelation. Natural revelation takes place when God introduces himself to humans through nature. It's the undeniable evidence of the divine through the splendor and grandeur of the created world. David gave us a perfect definition of natural revelation in Psalm 97:6: "The heavens proclaim his righteousness, and all the peoples see his glory."

But God wasn't finished with revelation. He wasn't through explaining himself to us. As we discussed in chapter 2, God has been revealing himself to the minds of humans since Adam and Eve, and therefore humans learned more and more about his divine nature. But these serendipitous visits of God were still limited in nature. The writer of Hebrews opened his epistle declaring, "In the past God spoke to our forefathers through the prophets at many times and in various ways" (Heb. 1:1). From the time of Adam and Eve to the prophet Malachi, God spoke to his people through dreams, visions, and prophetic messages. He was gradually revealing his nature and heart to the people he created and governed. But these revelations were only partial. They never told the whole story about God. The wording of Hebrews 1:1

127

implies that there was something unfinished or incomplete about the revelations of God to the Israelite forefathers.

But the limited revelations of God ended in a manger outside Bethlehem.

Two thousand years ago the revealing work of God came to a crescendo. The partial picture of God shown through natural revelation gave way to the ultimate revealing of God: Jesus Christ. When Jesus came to earth and lived among us, everything humans would ever need to know about God became accessible and even tangible. The biblical writer John summed up this special revelation of God through Jesus in the prologue to his Gospel: "No one has ever seen God. But the unique One, who is himself God, is near to the Father's heart. He has revealed God to us" (John 1:18 NLT).

One of my favorite Norman Rockwell paintings is called *Triple Self-Portrait.* It's a humorous and colorful attempt by the artist to capture himself on canvas. It shows the difficulty the artist had of being both the subject and the source of a painting.

God had no such difficulty. When he wanted the world to know what he looked like, he gave us Jesus. Were God to paint a portrait of himself, the image on the canvas would be of Jesus. If God were to snap a photo of himself with a digital camera, the image on the camera's screen would be of Jesus.

Jesus removed all the guesswork for us to know God. He made the constant flow of information and stimuli from God to the human mind manageable. Imagine a funnel. It's wide at the top and narrow at the bottom. It allows a substance to be poured into a container at a slow and manageable rate. The reality of God is overwhelming for us; in fact, it's infinite. But Jesus, in true funnel fashion, presented the information about God in a manner and at a pace we could understand. He is the ultimate, specific, and special revelation of God.

Do you remember what the second of the Ten Commandments is? It forbids us from making or worshiping any image and calling it God. Have you ever wondered why God was concerned with that? Besides the obvious foolishness of creating something and then calling it God, there was a more subtle reason for this command. God can't be captured by any image. Any attempt we make to reproduce or represent God in an image, no matter how noble or grand the effort, inevitably reduces him. It lessens him. An infinite God can't be captured or represented adequately by anything we create. So God commanded us not to even try. He told us that sunrises and sunsets, mountains and oceans, stars and comets, rivers and flowers, were sufficient communicators of his nature.

Until Jesus. When Jesus came along, everything changed. No longer did we have to wonder what God looked like. Jesus gave us firsthand exposure to the reality of God. He was the power, love, and holiness of God packed into human form. The apostle Paul could not have said it any more clearly: "He [Jesus] is the image of the invisible God" (Col. 1:15).

That's why I told Todd to look to Jesus. That's why I regularly tell agnostics and atheists who are still open to the possibility of God to think about the implications of Jesus's life and teachings. Jesus has a way of opening people's eyes to God when they otherwise can't see him.

Meet the Biblical Jesus

Before we discuss any further *why* it makes good sense to believe in and follow Jesus (which we will do in the next chapter), we need to acknowledge *what* specifically we believe about him. If we are going to counter the claims that Christ is insignificant, we need to know the reasons for his significance. Here is a summary of the biblical teachings about the person of Jesus.

- *Jesus is eternal.* John 1:1 claims that Jesus coexisted with God in eternity. He wasn't created and doesn't have a beginning to his existence. He is not bound by the limits of time. When he became man, he stepped into time for thirty-three brief years, but his true nature is eternal. To believe in Jesus is to believe in an eternally existing Savior.

- *Jesus is unique.* Isaiah the prophet predicted that Jesus would arrive on earth through a rather unusual path, and Matthew and Luke both confirmed this. While born to a young woman, Mary, Jesus had not been conceived through the typical human means. Mary was a virgin when she gave birth; Jesus was conceived in her by the power of God's Holy Spirit (see Isa. 7:14; Matt. 1:18–25; and Luke 1:26–38). This was a critical aspect of Jesus's nature, making him both fully human (via Mary) and fully divine (via God). To believe in Jesus is to believe in a Savior who is both God and man.

- *Jesus is reason and logic personified.* John used the popular Greek term *logos* as a name for Jesus (see John 1:1). While most English versions of the Bible translate *logos* as "word," there's much more to the Greek meaning. The Greeks thought *logos* to be a high and lofty concept. It included the idea of ultimate reason, wisdom, or intellect. When John claimed that Jesus was the *logos* of God, he was arguing that God's wisdom and knowledge had become human in the person of

Jesus Christ. Faith in Jesus includes the belief that he is the personification of God's wisdom.

- *Jesus is creative.* The Scriptures build an overwhelming case for the work of Jesus in creation. The verbs *spoke* or *said* are used repeatedly to describe how God created the earth: "God said, 'Let there be light'" (Gen. 1:3). God spoke and the heavens were made. The Old Testament repeatedly claims that the earth was created by God's word (see Gen. 1:3, 6, 9, 11, 14, 20, 24, 26; Pss. 33:6, 9; and 148:5). In the New Testament we learn that the creative Word of God is Jesus. John declared, "All things came into being through Him [the *logos*, God's Word], and apart from Him [the *logos*] nothing came into being that has come into being" (John 1:3 NASB). Both the apostle Paul and the writer of Hebrews declared that Jesus was not only the source of all creation but also its sustainer (see Col. 1:16–17 and Heb. 1:2–3). The Christian faith includes the belief that the Jesus who died on the cross for our sins is the powerful being who created the universe.

- *Jesus is divine.* Seven hundred years before Christ's birth, Isaiah predicted that the promised Messiah to the Hebrews would be the mighty God and eternal Father who would rule an everlasting kingdom (see Isa. 9:6–7). Perhaps the most definitive case made by the New Testament writers about Jesus was that he was, in fact, God in the flesh. As the philosopher John declared, "No one has seen God at any time; the only begotten God who is in the bosom of the Father, He has explained Him" (John 1:18 NASB).[1] In other words, God is an unexplainable, unsolvable mystery. No one can see him or approach him. So when God wanted to be known, he sent the final revelation of himself, Jesus

Christ, to earth. Jesus did more than just show us God, he modeled God for us. To believe in Jesus is to believe in the God who became flesh.

- *Jesus is the only way to God.* If Jesus is just one of many great and prophetic voices of God, then his claims of being the only way to God seem ludicrous and outrageous. If he is, however, the God-man, God incarnate, then his claims, although difficult and challenging, make sense. The Christian faith does not hesitate to present Jesus as the solution for the problem of sin, the agent of God's forgiveness to man, and the means of access through which people can get to God (see John 3:3, 16, 18; 11:25; 12:46; 14:6; and Rom. 3:21–26). Scandalous though it may be, the Christian message asserts that God has provided the only way for people to know him and find his mercy, and that way is through the life, death, and resurrection of the God-man, Jesus Christ.

While you may not fully understand all of these important points, it is critical that you at least know they are part of the Christian gospel. Don't succumb to the temptation of watering down the Christian faith to make it more palatable to skeptics. The uniqueness and edginess of Christ's message are part of what make it believable. Think about it—the Christian gospel and the faith it requires is nothing that any man or group of men would ever think up on their own. Surely no group of people intending to start a religion would ever dream up a story of God becoming man through the means of a virgin birth, of him dying for sins and offering grace over against religious works, and then tag the title of God onto a crucified and rejected Jew. And yet that's precisely what Christianity claims. That's one of the main reasons that I believe the Christian message—it's obvious that no person would ever come up with such a plan. Paul observed, "For the foolishness of God is wiser than man's wisdom, and the weakness of God is stronger than man's strength" (1 Cor. 1:25).

There is one additional attribute of Jesus that we need to consider, and it deals directly with the overall subject of this book. The Bible asserts that it is impossible to have true wisdom and knowledge without first seeking God (see Ps. 111:10; Prov. 1:7; 2:5; 9:10), and that the wisdom and knowledge of God were actually personified in Jesus Christ. Thus, if you want to be a real thinker, you have to believe in Jesus. Let's consider how Jesus and wisdom are connected.

Can I Interest You in an Apple?

Do you know what the oldest temptation in the world is? Most people think of power, sex, or money. Those temptations are certainly common and timeless. But if you think back to Eden, and if you consider what Satan lured Eve with, it wasn't power, sex, or money. Moses, the writer of Genesis, recorded for us what Eve was attracted to in the forbidden fruit: "When the woman saw that the fruit of the tree was good for food and pleasing to the eye, and also desirable for gaining wisdom, she took some and ate it. She also gave some to her husband, who was with her, and he ate it" (Gen. 3:6).

Did you note that the fruit was "desirable for gaining wisdom"? Satan promised Eve that she would be like God, knowing good and evil. At the core of Satan's temptation to the first couple was the allure of knowledge and wisdom. Why were those things attractive? Because with knowledge and wisdom came independence from God. If Adam and

Eve knew what God did, if they could answer the questions and solve the mysteries of the eternal, then they wouldn't need God. So they ate the fruit, and we've been paying for it ever since. Instead of becoming like God, Adam and Eve were thrust into chaos. Satan snared the first humans with the oldest trick in the book: know what God knows, and you won't need him.

In the New Testament, we find that Satan was still tempting people with knowledge. The apostle Paul wrote his letter to the ancient Greek city of Colossae in part to combat a popular heretical set of beliefs commonly known as Gnosticism. Named after the Greek word for "knowledge," Gnosticism promoted a philosophy and system of spiritual progressions that were based solely on human understanding. According to Gnosticism, the more people learned and knew, the more progress they made spiritually. The highest levels of spiritual existence were available only to those who reached them through learning. Faith in God wasn't part of the equation at all. The mind was no longer the place where people processed the information that God was making known; it was the tool they used to discover the secrets of God through their own thinking. Gnosticism was nothing more than the temptation of Eden wrapped up in a first-century-BC package.

Today Satan is still luring people away from God with the same trick. What's the primary appeal of atheism, agnosticism, and humanism today? Knowledge. People are called to embrace reason and intellect and thus to reject God. We're told that if we're smart enough, we won't need God. We're told that faith is foolish and that the future and hope of the world rest in great learning and sharp minds, not faith in something divine. And tragically, while these so-called intellects (one group actually uses the name "Brights" to describe themselves) claim to do away with the need for God through their own great thinking, they're actually falling for the oldest con in history.

A Real Wise Guy

What is true wisdom? What is real knowledge? Is it possible, as our culture clearly asserts, to have true knowledge without a relationship with God? Not according to the Bible.

You might be surprised to know that in the Bible, wisdom is given almost godlike properties. Consider some of these attributes assigned to wisdom by Old Testament writers:

- Wisdom has its source in God. "To God belong wisdom and power; counsel and understanding are his" (Job 12:13).
- Wisdom begins with fearing and honoring God. "The fear of the LORD is the beginning of wisdom; all who follow his precepts have good understanding" (Ps. 111:10).
- Wisdom is given by God and flows from his mouth. "For the LORD gives wisdom, and from his mouth come knowledge and understanding" (Prov. 2:6).
- God created the earth through his wisdom. "He made the earth by his power; he founded the world by his wisdom and stretched out the heavens by his understanding" (Jer. 51:15).
- Wisdom keeps us from evil. "Wisdom will save you from the ways of wicked men, from men whose words are perverse" (Prov. 2:12).

- Wisdom is more valuable than riches. "Blessed is the man who finds wisdom, the man who gains understanding, for she is more profitable than silver and yields better returns than gold. She is more precious than rubies; nothing you desire can compare with her" (Prov. 3:13–15).

- Wisdom should be sought above everything else. "Wisdom is supreme; therefore get wisdom. Though it cost all you have, get understanding" (Prov. 4:7).

In Proverbs 8, the writer Solomon gave what is probably the loftiest description of wisdom in the Old Testament. And yet, as we look at the New Testament, Solomon could have just as easily been describing Jesus Christ. Consider the following comparisons:

Wisdom in Proverbs 8	Jesus in the New Testament
Wisdom seeks a relationship with all people (vv. 1–11)	Jesus wants all people to come to him (John 6:37)
All who seek wisdom will find it (v. 17)	All who seek Christ will find him (Matt. 7:7; John 3:16; 6:37)
Wisdom is eternal (vv. 22–23)	Jesus is eternal (John 1:1–2; Col. 1:15)
Wisdom partnered with God in creation (vv. 27–31)	Jesus partnered with God in creation (John 1:3; Col. 1:16)
Blessing is found in following wisdom (vv. 32–34)	Blessing is found in following Jesus (John 8:12)
Whoever finds wisdom finds life (v. 35)	Whoever finds Jesus finds life (Matt. 10:39; John 3:15–16)
Whoever rejects wisdom loses life (v. 36)	Whoever rejects Jesus loses life (John 3:18, 36)

The similarities between wisdom in the Old Testament and Jesus in the New Testament are no coincidence. The New Testament writers clearly saw Jesus as the personification of God's divine attributes. Solomon's concept of the holy, creating, life-giving wisdom of God became flesh and walked among us as Jesus Christ (see John 1:14, 18).

The apostle Paul provided a sweeping summary statement of the connection between wisdom and Jesus when he wrote, "My purpose is that they may be encouraged in heart and united in love, so that they may have the full riches of complete understanding, in order that they may know the mystery of God, namely, Christ, in whom are hidden all the treasures of wisdom and knowledge" (Col. 2:2–3).

Did you catch some common themes there? *Mystery, understanding, knowledge, wisdom,* and *Christ.* In the minds of the biblical writers, those themes are inseparable. The mystery of God has been revealed—his knowledge and wisdom have become fully available through Christ. Jesus doesn't just give us access to God, he gives us access to God's mind. As Paul wrote, "It is because of him [God] that you are in Christ Jesus, who has become for us wisdom from God—that is, our righteousness, holiness and redemption" (1 Cor. 1:30).

This Is Your Brain on Sin. Any Questions?

If the Bible's claims about Jesus are true, then what are the implications for thinking people? What conclusions can we draw from the message of Christ?

First, *the human brain is designed to believe.* God didn't create an insurmountable Mount Everest of faith that seekers must scale in order to know him. Rather, he asks truth-seeking people only to do what comes naturally to the human mind—believe. Hebrews 11:6 tells us that without faith it is impossible to please God. Faith, while initially challenging for many, doesn't have to remain elusive. Job declared, "It is the spirit in a man, the breath of the Almighty, that gives him understanding" (Job 32:8). Simply put, God is ready and willing to come to the aid of those who *want* to believe. He will help truth seekers understand him and the message of his Son. Every person's brain is perfectly equipped to think on the high level that faith requires.

Second, *Christian faith is the fulfillment of the human mind*. Rather than being an intellectual hindrance, faith in Christ is actually an intellectual stimulant. When sin entered the world, men and women lost the capacity to think on the high levels that God intended. Our reasoning capacities were blunted and thwarted by the fog of sin. The command that Jesus taught as one of the most important—to love God with all your mind—became impossible. In Romans 1, Paul argued that all who reject the knowledge of God actually have depraved or morally inept minds (see v. 28). But through Christ, God begins the work of restoring our minds to their pre-sin splendor. We regain some of our original ability to think on the high and holy levels that God intended. That's why Paul commanded believers to "take captive every thought" under Christ (2 Cor. 10:5) and to think about things that are pure, holy, lovely, and praiseworthy (see Phil. 4:8). Part of the promise of the gospel is that the human mind will eventually be restored to the level of beauty and sophistication that it lost in Eden. The Holy Spirit begins this restoration process in us here on earth and completes it in heaven (see Phil. 1:6).

Third, *people who reject Jesus have been intellectually and mentally blinded*. In 2 Corinthians 4:4, Paul offers sobering insight into the mental and intellectual condition of those who reject Christ: "The god of this age has blinded the minds of unbelievers, so that they cannot see the light of the gospel of the glory of Christ, who is the image of God." Paul attributes unbelievers' lack of faith, at least in part, to the work of "the god of this age." Satan, the author of all lies, has rendered unbelievers blind and incapable of seeing the truth of Christ. But did you notice what he blinded? Their minds. The rational, reasonable elements of belief simply escape their grasp. That's why so many skeptics accuse believers of not thinking. To them, faith looks irrational. They're blind to the truth of God. But the implication of Paul's teaching couldn't be any clearer: if people are to know God, then they are going to have to include their minds in the process.

Why Faith Makes Sense

Because Jesus was God in the flesh, he became the ultimate way for all people to truly know God. As the special revelation of God, Jesus determined the means by which humans could relate to and be forgiven by God. But there is another equally profound thing that happened in the special revelation of Jesus Christ. When Jesus made God accessible, he made God's wisdom accessible as well. He made the heart and mind of God available to humans. Jesus is the ultimate proof of why it's not foolish to be a person of faith. From the Bible's standpoint, our minds can't reach their highest potential until they have been enlightened by Christ. Rather than blunting our thinking capacities, faith in Jesus actually enhances them.

9

Name Above All Names

The red-faced actor, a well-known comedian, screamed into the camera: "Be healed! In Jesus's name, come out! Demon, come out!" His on-screen counterpart, a child actor, joined in: "Christ's power compels you! Christ's power compels you! Come out of him!" The two repeatedly beat their twentysomething victim on the head with a Bible and their fists. All of this religious activity was presented in an effort to heal the young man of a simple bloody nose. The movie was a comedy. I didn't think it was funny. The intended jab at Christians, and more importantly, our Savior, was obvious.

Why is it that Jesus so quickly draws the harshest ire of society? Why is it so popular and culturally acceptable to criticize, lampoon, redefine, attack, and mock Jesus? Whether it's the merely human Jesus of *The Da Vinci Code*, complete with wife and kids; the lustful, adulterous Jesus of *The Last Temptation of Christ*, who fantasizes while hanging on the cross about having sex with Mary Magdalene; the weak and emasculated Jesus created by the Jesus Seminar;[1] the evolved Man Jesus of Mormonism; or the historically fictional Jesus as claimed by a small number of atheists, Jesus remains a popular bull's-eye for many individuals' angry outbursts.

Recently, comedian Kathy Griffin won an Emmy for her reality show, *My Life on the D-List.* In her acceptance speech, Griffin noted that award winners often thank or acknowledge Jesus for helping them win their award. But not her. Griffin bragged that Jesus had nothing to do with her good fortune. She said that if Jesus had gotten his way, some other comedian would have won. She then made such a disparaging and offensive statement about Jesus that the network wouldn't air it, held up the statue, and said, "This award is my god now."[2] As if that wasn't enough, an atheist group created a website and started a petition-signing campaign in support of the comedian's comments.

In our culture today, Jesus's name is thrown around not just with a casual flippancy but often with venom and disdain. In fact, I'm sure Jesus's name is slandered much more frequently and consistently and treated with more disrespect than any other name in history. Have you ever wondered, *Why is that?*

It is, quite simply, because Jesus is the eye of the storm in the issue of the credibility of Christianity. His nature and identity are ground zero in the battle that is being fought over whether Christians can be taken seriously. If Jesus can be proven to be false, a fraud, or even fictional, then the entire Christian faith will crumble into dust.

The controversial message of Jesus's teachings and the narrow and exclusive nature of his claims make him a great target for anyone looking to find easier, more palatable paths to God. Think about it—what sophisticated, self-respecting person wants to believe in a God who slaughtered his own

Son in response to his or her own human shortcomings? The hard-line message of the Christian gospel and its claims to have a monopoly on the way to God make it very offensive to many.

But beyond that, there is something else going on. Simply stated, Jesus's message is true, and the devil knows it. Jesus gets assaulted and slandered because he is at the heart of the battle for the souls of men and women. Were Jesus truly insignificant, he wouldn't get the negative airtime he so easily attracts.

So what do you think? Are you crazy to believe in Jesus? Is it an intellectually wise decision to follow Christ? Let's find out.

Why Skeptics Reject Jesus

If you've ever had conversations with unbelievers about why they don't believe, they may offer any number of reasons. Some don't believe in Jesus's miraculous birth; others doubt his resurrection. Some have issues with the veracity of the Bible or with Jesus's ability to perform miracles. Others will tell you that his message is simply too offensive or outlandish to be believable.

But the reasons for accepting Christ's claims are both numerous and persuasive. His life in Palestine two thousand years ago, his death under Jewish and Roman condemnation, and the explosive birth and growth of his movement after his death are historically verifiable facts. Add to these the four different eyewitness accounts of Jesus's life and ministry provided in the Gospels; the extraordinarily high level of documentation and textual accuracy of the New Testament; the numerous Hebrew messianic prophecies fulfilled by Jesus; the multiple eyewitnesses who claim to have seen, heard, talked with, touched, and dined with Jesus after his death and resurrection; and history's inability to offer a meaningful counter to the claims of Jesus's resurrection or to produce his dead body; and you've got an undeniably compelling case for the truth of Christ's message.

Many other skeptics, though not all, base their decision to deny Christ on flimsy or flat-out wrong data. Much like Jesus's opponents mentioned in the New Testament, many unbelievers today just don't have their facts straight. The next time you meet someone who says he doesn't believe in Jesus, ask how much research into Jesus he has actually done. You'll find that few have ever engaged in any real serious thinking about him.

The Claim That Jesus Is the Only Way to God

There may be no aspect of the Christian faith more offensive, and no reason for people's rejection of it more quoted, than the claim that Jesus alone can lead people to God. I can't count the number of conversations I've had with skeptics who patently refuse to believe in Christianity, regardless of its merits, because they feel like they don't have any choice in how they get to heaven. Our "have it your way" culture doesn't like not having options, even with eternity at stake. We're proud and self-reliant enough to expect God to give us a multiple-choice plan.

So when Jesus said, "I am the way and the truth and the life. No one comes to the Father except through me" (John 14:6), he started a firestorm of controversy that has lasted over two thousand years. But what he did *not* do was present a compelling argument for rejecting him. His claim to be the only legitimate route to God may be offensive to the more independent thinkers in society, but it doesn't make it any less true. As God incarnate, Jesus had a perspective that we don't have on what is required to know God. In fact, he has the *only* perspective on what is required. As the designer of his plan of salvation, God determined the means by which he is to be known. Just because I don't like or agree with that means doesn't make it any less viable. It simply shows that I'm too proud to walk through the door God has opened for me. God is not inclined to rewire eternity just to fit my preferences.

Suppose you approach a building and you notice that it has only one entrance. Years or even decades before you arrived at the building, an architect determined the most reasonable means of entrance and exit to the facility. The building was built based on that design. If you get to the building and decide you don't like where the door is, you don't call up the architect and ask him or her to redesign the building or relocate the door. You would be told, probably not in very polite terms, to either get over it or go elsewhere. Your demands for special treatment would be ludicrous.

But when it comes to God, when it comes to dealing with the Creator of the universe and the source of every breath we draw, we somehow think it permissible to argue with him about the means he established for us to get to heaven—a means, by the way, that cost him the life of his Son.

Jesus Christ is the only way to God because he alone was in a position to remove that which separated us from God in the first place—our sin. When Jesus died his vicarious death on the cross, he didn't just *create* the way to God (much like an architect would create a point of ingress), he *became* the way to God. There's nothing unfair or exclusive about Jesus providing the only access to God. On the contrary, in his death he has done for us what we could never do for ourselves. Jesus has actually given a means of spiritual CPR to a dying race. All a person must do is receive it and be made whole. There's nothing to work for, nothing to earn, nothing to purchase. The entire process of seeking and finding God is made possible by Jesus.

What about People Who Have Never Heard of Jesus?

Without exception, the most common and troubling question about Christianity is that of the eternal future of those who have not heard of Jesus Christ. Believers and unbelievers alike wrestle with Jesus's apparent condemnation of any and all who don't know him. Such wrestling indeed seems justified. With statements such as, "Whoever believes in the Son has eternal life, but whoever rejects the Son will not see life, for God's wrath remains on him" (John 3:36) and "I am the way and the truth and the life. No one comes to the Father except through me" (John 14:6), it's easy to draw the conclusion that God is calloused toward those who haven't had the chance to know of Jesus. Readers of the New Testament who are looking for a reason to reject Christianity find plenty of ammo in verses like these. The apparent hypocrisy of God is obvious: he claims to be loving, generous, and grace filled, but in the next breath he declares that if someone happens to be so unfortunate as to be born in a land or time in which Christ is not known, then his or her soul is in peril. Without proper interpretation, such verses are more than enough to cause a seeker to look elsewhere.

But God is loving, generous, and grace filled, and he does not doom people to eternal perdition by nature of their birthplace or the time of history in which they were born. If we're going to know that Christianity makes sense rationally, and if we're going to be able to set at ease the minds of those who struggle with this apparent callousness of God, then we need to come to terms with what the New Testament teaches about how people are judged by God. The good news is that we already know part of the answer.

To begin with, let's acknowledge the difference between not hearing about Jesus and rejecting Jesus. It is not a sin to have never heard of and therefore not believe in Jesus. God does not hold people accountable for what they don't know; he holds them accountable for what they do know. It is sinful and the ultimate display of poor judgment to hear about Christ and his sacrificial death and then reject him. Jesus spoke of this when he said, "Whoever believes in him is not condemned, but whoever does not believe stands condemned already because he has not believed in the name of God's one and only Son" (John 3:18). Jesus said that people were judged not for their ignorance of him but rather for their rejection of him.

In John 14:6, Jesus made the definitive theological statement about his role in bringing people throughout history to God. Unfortunately, his words are often poorly interpreted and have been used for centuries to turn people away from the gospel. When Jesus said, "I am the way and the truth and the life. No one comes to the Father except through me," he was *not* saying that those who never hear of him are immediately condemned. In fact, his statement doesn't even address the eternal condition of those who don't hear about him. Jesus was simply stating the critical role he plays in making access to God available. He was saying that if people are going to come to God, then they're going to have to come through the means God established.

When people believe in and yield to Jesus, the effect of Jesus's death on the cross—forgiveness, mercy, and the removal of sin—is applied to them by God. They are declared holy and adopted forever as God's children. They have come to God through the means Jesus made possible. Jesus has indeed become the way to God for them. But when people hear of Jesus and reject his claims, they also reject the only means God has provided through which their sins can be forgiven. They have come to the building but rejected the door. With no means of forgiveness open to them, they will be judged for their sins and punished accordingly.

For people who hear of Jesus and choose to either accept or reject him, the basis for their eternal status is rather cut-and-dried. Their judgment is based on their response to the special revelation of Jesus in their lives. But what about those who have never heard of Jesus? What about people who live or have lived in places not blessed with churches, missionaries, or Bibles? How does God judge them? And what about all the billions of people who lived *before* Jesus? They had no chance to experience God's grace. There was no Bible for them to read, no church to preach the gospel to them, no missionary to take the Good News to them. How were they saved? How can Jesus possibly be the only way to God for people who never knew he existed?

I hinted earlier that you already know the answer to this difficult question. It's found in the concept we've already discussed at length—*revelation*. Here's an important principle to know when wrestling with the question of what happens to people who have never heard of Jesus: *people are accountable for the revelation of God that they receive.*

People raised in Christ-honoring homes or in Western cultures with churches on every corner and Bibles in every bookstore have a very high level of revelation from God. They know about Christ and have sufficient opportunity to believe in him. They will be judged by how they respond to him.

But people who have never heard of Christ can't be judged the same way. Their revelation of God is different. Rather than being held accountable for their awareness of Jesus (which they don't have), they are held accountable for their awareness of God. And, as we learned in earlier chapters, every person alive has an overwhelming awareness of God. The Psalms in the Old Testament and Romans 1 in the New Testament make it clear that the case for God as revealed in nature is undeniable. Even if a man or woman lives on a deserted island and never comes into contact with another human, he or she has all the information necessary to come into a saving relationship with God. Much like Abram's faith in Genesis 15:6, that person's faith in and humility before God is "credited . . . to him as righteousness."

When a person humbly acknowledges God, I believe the effect of Jesus's blood is applied to them. They may have never heard of Jesus or been aware of his death on the cross, but through their humble acknowledgment of and submission to the God of creation, the saving grace of Jesus's death is applied to them. I believe that Jesus becomes the way to God for that person, even though they have never heard of Jesus's death for their sins. And the Scriptures clearly teach that there is enough evidence of God in creation to lead every human to a correct and saving conclusion about God.

Jethro, the Midianite father-in-law of Moses, became a priest and worshiper of the God of Israel. When Jesus died on the cross 1,300 years later, the power of his blood was applied to Jethro. He became the way to God for him. When Rahab, a harlot who lived in the pagan and godless city of Jericho, humbled herself and sought the favor of the God of Israel, Jesus became the way to God for her. And when the people of Nineveh, a ruthless Assyrian city, repented and sought the God of Israel after hearing the preaching of Jonah, Jesus became the way to God for them.

All throughout history, men and women have been judged by God based on the revelation they have of him. As people humbly respond to that revelation, Jesus's blood is applied to them. Their humility and repentance is credited to them as righteousness (see Gen. 15:6). Jesus's statement in John 14:6 tells us how they get to God: they walk down the road, or enter through the door, that Jesus opened for them. There really is no other way to God.

The Fine Print

There are, however, some obvious conditions and limits to the access Jesus provides to God. Tragically, not everyone who believes in God (see James 2:19) or a god is going to heaven. In defending and articulating our faith, we need to be able to explain what limits exist and why. Here are some broad descriptions of the types of people who miss the way Jesus provides to God.

- *Those who hear about Jesus and reject him.* Unfortunately, Western culture is filled with people who know of the claims of Christ and reject them. People who hear of Jesus have the highest level of God's revelation available to humans. No clearer or more powerful presentation of the nature, love, and grace of God exists. For people to hear of Christ and reject his claims is to seal their fate for eternity. Judgment and just condemnation await those who openly reject Christ.
- *Those who believe in God but think he can be bribed.* Some people seek to negotiate with or manipulate God. Many people around the world and throughout history

have come to the correct conclusion that a creating God exists. But rather than humbling themselves before him and seeking his mercy, they seek to bribe or appease him through religious practices, behaviors, or sacrifices. The clear message about God in nature is that he is holy, infinite, and awesome, and he cannot be bought (see Isaiah 40). To try to bribe or appease him is to treat him as a peer, or at least as something less than a holy God. When an Aztec offers his son as a human sacrifice, or a Muslim attempts to gain favor with God by keeping the five major tenets of Islam, both miss the point entirely. The God revealed in sunrises and sunsets can only be worshiped and exalted, not negotiated with. "For the LORD your God is God of gods and Lord of lords, the great God, mighty and awesome, who shows no partiality and accepts no bribes" (Deut. 10:17).

• *Those who try to dodge the issue.* Some people reason that if they don't vote for or against Jesus, then they can't be held accountable for their decision. Their plan for dealing with Jesus is *not* to deal with him, thus somehow trapping God into owing them a pass into eternity on the technical loophole that they didn't actually ever reject Jesus.

Captain Chris is a great example of such thinking. Captain Chris runs a boat charter business on the tiny island of Port Aransas, Texas. I met him while on a retreat with a few church staff members. Chris is a rough and rowdy character with an opinion about everything. He seemed like a great candidate to lure into a conversation about spiritual matters, so I threw him some bait. Chris didn't disappoint me, and we quickly found ourselves in a lively conversation.

Chris refused to be nailed down on the issue of Jesus. He felt that Jesus was a great idea for those who needed or wanted him, but he thought he wasn't one of those people. He wasn't opposed to Christ and his message, but he refused to acknowledge that there was anything valid about Jesus. When I asked Chris what he thought God would say to him when he stood before him, he replied, "Nothing. But I know what I'll say to God. The first words out of my mouth will be, 'See, I told you I was right.'" I remember feeling the distinct need to back up, lest the lightning bolts certain to come hit me by accident.

There are no special cases or unique privileges when dealing with the God of the universe. We will meet God on his terms and turf, not ours. There are no loopholes or escape clauses that allow us to worm our way out of being fully accountable to God. When we stand before him, if we are indeed allowed to say anything, it will be to simply confess the lordship of Jesus Christ (see Phil. 2:9–11).

- *Those who redefine God.* This group makes the God of creation into something less than holy and infinite, thereby removing their need to humble themselves before him. Many Mormons believe that God is simply an evolved man. Many Buddhists claim that God is part of a pantheon of other gods, all of whom they can gain access to and even become part of through reincarnation and good works. Hindus have a very diverse belief system, which can include the belief in one god, many gods, or no god at all. People who seek to redefine God clearly reject his revelation through nature. In doing so, they also miss the way that Jesus has made available to them.

Jesus Christ is not one of many ways to God. He is the *only* way to God. But the reality of Christ as the way to God isn't nearly as scandalous as it has been made to appear by our faith's critics. While it is true that Christianity teaches that a person can only be humble before God, rather than try to impress or appease him, it does not claim that God just casts off for eternity those who have not been fortunate enough to hear of his Son. Tragically, many throughout history and even today have rejected the obvious revelation of God through nature, thus disqualifying themselves from his saving grace. But God, rather than being the eternal brute and thug our culture has painted him as, is actually a benevolent and gracious deity who has gone to extremes to make sure that we all have the chance to know him—including the extreme of sacrificing his own Son.

A Good Investment

So is faith in Jesus reasonable? Does it make good intellectual and rational sense to stake one's eternity on the claims of Christ? Absolutely. Here are four realities that make faith in Jesus a good investment.

The Resurrection

"Big news was broken yesterday: Jesus and his family have been found dead in their graves in Israel. . . . Brace yourself. James Cameron, the man who brought you *The Titanic*, is back with another blockbuster. This time, the ship he's sinking is Christianity."[3] You may have read or heard about this claim or countless others like it. Interestingly, as I write this paragraph several months after Cameron's supposed discovery, it's already old news. Jesus's resurrection, despite Hollywood's and pseudoscience's best efforts to discredit it, remains a historical fact.

The credibility of the Christian message really does live or die on the resurrection of Jesus. The Bible does not propose a symbolic or spiritual resurrection of Christ. The biblical writers asserted and went to their graves believing that their leader had indeed come back from the dead physically and had confirmed it by appearing to them over the next forty days.

It is difficult to account for the radical change in demeanor and behavior not just of Peter but of all the disciples and early followers of Christ, but for the fact that they saw, talked to, dined with, and touched the resurrected Jesus. Otherwise, their transition from cowering behind locked doors in secret to boldly preaching Christ in the temple is nearly impossible to explain. It's been two millennia since the claims of Jesus's resurrection were first presented to the world. Those claims have remained solidly intact and immovable in the face of every attack, test, theory, and lie offered up to undermine them. The reality of Jesus's resurrection from the dead makes your faith in Christ intellectually sound.[4]

The Existence of the Church

The two-thousand-year presence of the Christian church on earth is another great reason to trust the viability of the Christian message. Think about it—when the brutal Roman emperor Nero declared all-out war on Christians, arresting, torturing, and killing significant numbers of them, which would you have bet on to survive: the Roman Empire or the church? But within just a few centuries of Nero's reign, Rome fell and the church continued to prevail.

Jesus left his movement in the hands of no more than 120 mostly untrained, mostly uneducated, and relatively poor Jewish men and women. Yet in the face of unyielding spiritual, political, economic, and physical oppression, the movement of Jesus not only survived, but it also thrived and became the world's most prolific, dominant, and influential belief system. The only meaningful way to account for such success is that the movement started by Jesus is, in fact, true and backed by the very power of God.

As I travel to other nations—specifically, highly impoverished ones—or when I read the accounts of Christ-followers from places like China and India, I am joyfully reminded that the church of Jesus is indeed alive and well around the world. The torch of Christ isn't going out. It is successfully being passed from one generation to the next. And all the efforts of governments, scholars, scientists, other religions, atheists, and even Satan to quench the fire of the church serve only to enflame and spread it. Consider the existence of the Christian church and know that your faith in Christ makes good sense.

Life Change

For two thousand years, the message of Christ has had the uncanny ability to change lives. Whether it is the transformation of the fearful, cowering disciples into bold Christian proclaimers in the days after the resurrection; the sacrifice of martyrs, past and present, who willingly endure torture and death for Christ; or the countless millions in history who have abandoned riches, fame, power, and sin to embrace the disciplined, yielded life of following Christ, it is difficult to explain away Jesus's ability to apprehend, redirect, and empower lives. Where well-intended recovery programs, the threat of social rejection, and even criminal prosecution have been unable to halt immoral and unethical behavior, the gospel of Jesus has an unmatched success rate in turning sinners into saints. History has seen no more effective agent of personal change than the message of Christ.

Consider Chuck Colson, the intelligent and articulate former Watergate conspirator who committed his life to Christ while in prison and subsequently founded one of the world's most effective prison ministries. And what about Norma McCorvey? She was Jane Roe in the landmark *Roe v. Wade* Supreme Court case that legalized abortion. After meeting a group of Christians in 1995, McCorvey became a Christ-follower, admitted to lying about being raped in her now-infamous *Roe v. Wade* testimony, and started a ministry called *Roe No More*, which shares the gospel of Christ and offers hope to those struggling with abortion issues.

Or consider my personal favorite, Larry. He was a thirty-eight-year-old alcoholic, cocaine addict, and homosexual who was HIV positive. After meeting a group of Christians in New Orleans during Mardi Gras, Larry embraced the claims of Christ and sought forgiveness for his sins. After kneeling on Bourbon Street in the French Quarter and yielding to Christ, Larry never again drank, snorted, injected, or had a sexual encounter of any kind. He remained sober, clean, and straight until his death several years later. Larry was, without exception, the most radical example of Christ's ability to change a life that I have ever seen.

History is filled with billions of stories like these. Nothing can account for the gospel's ability to change lives other than the fact that it is linked inseparably to the power of God. Jesus's transformation of people's lives is proof that your faith in him is a good investment.

Allure

One final reason to believe that the Christian faith is legitimate is the magnetic nature of Jesus. Jesus said, "But I, when I am lifted up from the earth, will draw all men to myself" (John 12:32). Jesus was speaking of his imminent crucifixion. He predicted that after he was "lifted up," he would indeed become the most alluring and highly charged religious figure in history. His prediction has proven true through the centuries. His name truly is a lightning rod in many cultures, his message the most debated throughout the ages.

Again, countless examples of Jesus's holy pull on people's lives can be found in the annals of history. Kings and priests, politicians and generals, stars and celebrities, and common people from all walks of life have been testifying to the allure of Jesus since he ascended to heaven two thousand years ago. For my purposes here, I'd like to offer an account that I personally witnessed.

Richard was a wealthy, powerful man who worked in the world of high-stakes politics. He was a consultant for some of the most well-known leaders in today's American political landscape. His religious upbringing left him more skeptical of faith than attracted to it. For years Richard considered himself an agnostic. But through the influence of many Christian friends, Richard never really closed the door on the possibility that Jesus's claims might be valid. One night, after being awakened at 1:30 a.m. by an unknown force, Richard felt moved to grab his Bible and read the Gospel of John. After hours of reading the account of Jesus's life and teachings, Richard, a twenty-first-century skeptic, knelt and gave his life to Jesus Christ.

I could tell a similar story over and over, with only the names changing—Angela, the thirty-year-old angry young woman; Manny, the sixty-year-old skeptical Jew; Dan, the thirty-year-old grieving widower; Linda, the forty-year-old manic depressive; Bill, the sixty-eight-year-old university scholar; Tim, the seventeen-year-old atheist. All had an encounter with Christ that they could neither avoid nor recover from. They felt his holy pull, heard his holy call, and answered. And each, to the glory of God, lives for Jesus today.

Very little can be offered as a reasonable explanation for the type of holy ambush that Richard and countless others have experienced at the hands of Christ. Jesus really is drawing all people to himself. As we stated earlier in the book, Jesus can be rejected, but he cannot be ignored. The sheer allure of his name throughout history proves that your faith in him is valid.

Why Faith Makes Sense

Jesus Christ is indeed ground zero of the most important battle in history. He is no fad, no mere movement, and no tidal current that ebbs and flows with the gravitational pull of culture. Jesus is the rock of history. As God's incarnate Son, he provided the way to God through which all people—past, present, and future—must come if they are to know God. The evidence for the validity of Jesus's existence, life, death, resurrection, ascension, and outpouring of his Spirit onto his church is overwhelming and has stood the test of history. Your faith in Jesus Christ makes good sense from every conceivable angle—historically, archaeologically, scientifically, psychologically, theologically, and spiritually. People who believe in Jesus aren't the mental duds of culture. Rather, they are the keepers of the light, the salt of the earth, the stars in the midst of darkness, and the agents of love to a dying world. You're not crazy to believe in Jesus. You would be crazy if you didn't.

10

A Beautiful Mind

It was any parent's worst nightmare. His twelve-year-old daughter was sick, very sick. In fact, she was dying. He had done everything he knew to help her. Doctors had been called in. The poor girl had endured many painful—and fruitless—treatments. Prayers and sacrifices had been offered. Nothing had helped. Jairus was desperate. His daughter was dying, and there was nothing he could do to stop it.

Then he heard that Jesus was nearby. Jairus knew about Jesus; at least, he had heard the stories about him. He knew that Jesus was a profound teacher, that he said things no one else dared to. He said things that no one else *could* say. But beyond that, Jairus had heard that Jesus actually healed people. He had heard of the blind regaining their sight, lame men walking, multitudes being fed miraculously. He had even heard that Jesus had stopped a funeral service outside the village of Nain and raised a dead man back to life. Who knew if those rumors were true? Yet they gave Jairus a glimmer of hope. What did he have to lose? So he set out to find Jesus.

Was Jairus's hope reasonable? Was it rational? On the one hand, it didn't make much sense for Jairus to hold out hope for his daughter when the best medical minds of his day had been unable to help her. Conventional wisdom would say Jairus's time would be better spent sitting at his daughter's bedside in her last few hours, not chasing after Jesus. On the other hand, Jairus had heard multiple reports about Jesus's abilities. Surely so many eyewitnesses and firsthand accounts couldn't *all* be wrong. Jairus went looking for Jesus based on the hope that what he had been told about him was true. No, it wasn't a completely rational move on Jairus's part, but neither was it completely irrational.

Jairus did find Jesus, and Luke tells us with crushing brevity that he was too late: "While Jesus was still speaking, someone came from the house of Jairus, the synagogue ruler. 'Your daughter is dead,' he said. 'Don't bother the teacher any more'" (Luke 8:49). Jairus's noble effort to save his daughter had failed. However reasonable his hope in Jesus's abilities may have been, all seemed lost now as Jairus dealt with the tragic news of his daughter's death. Imagine this father's heartache as he faced the knowledge that he had missed being with his daughter at her death because he was out trying to find some supposed miracle worker. I'm sure the skeptics had a lot to say: "If Jesus is so smart, why didn't he know Jairus was coming?" "Surely this miracle man could have just waved his hand and healed that girl." "What a waste. Can you believe Jairus even hoped in Jesus at all?"

Faith versus Reason

Imagine the shock and even disdain the skeptics must have felt when Jesus told Jairus not to lose hope. Luke's record of the event seems almost surreal: "Hearing this, Jesus said to Jairus, 'Don't be afraid; just believe, and she will be healed'" (Luke 8:50). What was Jesus thinking? How could he stare a grieving parent in the face and tell him to keep on believing?

Welcome to the classic collision between faith and reason. There is certainly no more immovable, impersonal, uncaring, and final force on the earth than death. When death has locked its icy grip on a life, nothing can reverse it. To even hint to a father about his dead daughter being healed seems nothing less than cruel. Given death's success rate and humans' inability to reverse death, Jesus's statement to Jairus, at least from a rational level, seems absurd. And yet there our Savior stood, with straight-faced sobriety, telling Jairus to keep on believing, even when every ounce of reason told him it would be irrational to do so.

What was going on in that exchange between Jairus and Jesus? Was Jesus really asking Jairus to think and believe irrationally? Was he asking him to set aside reason and embrace fanciful thinking? Or was Jesus calling Jairus to think on a higher level than he ever had before? To answer these questions and to equip us to move further into this discussion, we need to establish some working definitions. Let's start with *reason*.

Reason is simply using your mind to determine the logic or likeliness of an idea or proposal. A hypothesis or proposal is reasonable if existing evidence and previous experience seem to support it. If you come home to find your front door smashed in, your house ransacked, and several items missing, it is reasonable to conclude that your house has been broken into by thieves. Existing facts and previous experience would argue that the thief theory is a fairly safe conclusion. It would be unreasonable to conclude that aliens had landed in your front yard and broken into your house in search of something they could use to repair their malfunctioning spaceship. No evidence or experience exists to support such a strange hypothesis. Reason lives in the world of knowledge (what you know to be true) and experience (what you have personally experienced or know that others have experienced before).

Now, let's look at what is often cited as the antithesis of reason: *faith*. Here's my working definition: *faith* is simply using your mind to determine the logic or likeliness of an idea or proposal. No, that's not a misprint, and no, you're not confused. I gave you the exact same definition for faith that I did for reason, because initially, the two are exactly the same.

Faith has the same basic working ingredients as reason—knowledge and experience. The difference is that faith often extends into the invisible, intangible world, whereas reason is typically limited to only those things that are measurable and quantifiable.

I remember the first time I planned to snowshoe across a frozen lake in the winter. It was a huge lake I had hiked around many times before in the summer. But this time I would walk right across the middle of it. As I approached the lake, I wondered if the ice would be thick enough to support my weight. I saw that several inches of snow had accumulated on the lake's surface, and that the wind had blown some of the snow into drifts, revealing dark, solid sheets of ice. But most importantly, I saw the tracks of other hikers who had crossed the lake without any apparent incident. The combination of those three discoveries—the snow's accumulation, the exposed deep sheets of ice, and the tracks of those who had gone before me—led me to reason that it was safe to venture out across the lake. In fact, given the evidence before me, it would have been unreasonable to conclude that the lake was unsafe for crossing. That conclusion would have been driven by fear, not reason.

The relationship between faith and reason is similar. Even though we can't see or prove the existence of the invisible world around us, we can draw reasonable conclusions about it based on our experience and knowledge. As Christians, we have the Bible, filled with millennia-old promises and teachings about God and his desire to show his power in our daily lives. Christians and seekers alike have the reality of prayer and those strange coincidences/miracles that seem to occur quite frequently when we pray. We have the tracks of those who have gone before us—those men and women throughout history whose lives testify to their belief in and relationship with a power that is completely otherworldly. We have our own experiences—those moments of mental inspiration and illumination that we can't explain; those times of guilt and sorrow over bad things we've done, even those that no one else knows about; and those hair-raising encounters with a sunset, a thunderstorm, a field of flowers, a deep canyon, or a newborn baby—where we know in our gut that something, or someone, is behind them. It's not just that we're in awe of what we see, but we're in awe of the reality behind what we see that could cause it in the first place.

That combination of our knowledge and experience makes the belief in a realm that we can't see, and the governing power behind it, seem less irrational and more logical.

I tend to think that faith is very much like your relationship to a chair. You walk into a room and look for a place to sit. A chair in the corner catches your attention. As you approach it, your mind quickly and automatically runs a series of diagnostics about the chair: it looks sturdy, it resembles nearly every other chair you've sat in recently, it doesn't show any signs of weakness, and so on. Before you actually sit down, your mind tells you that based on your knowledge of chairs, the laws of physics, and your countless past experiences where chairs just like this one haven't failed you, it's safe to sit. But even with all that evidence and experience, it still takes faith to sit in the chair, because you will fall hard and fast if the chair fails. There's still faith involved, but faith that's based on the concepts of reason, knowledge, and experience.

Skeptics have tried to steal these concepts from those of us who believe, saying that reason, knowledge, and experience apply only to the material, observable world. They argue that faith in the invisible is foolish and that Christians are dunces for entertaining such intellectually bankrupt thinking. The skeptics are wrong, and we shouldn't sit quietly by while they steal concepts such as reason and logic from the lexicon of faith.

When Jesus challenged Jairus to keep on believing, he was asking him to extend reason to its next level. He asked Jairus to build on the foundation of what he knew and had heard about Jesus. That's what faith does. It builds on the platform of what we already know to be true of God in our relationship with him.

Faith is not the antithesis of reason. It is rather reason at its highest levels. Jesus asked Jairus to push past his intellectual fears and to step up to a higher level of thinking. It may not be *humanly* rational to believe that a dead girl can live, but it is *divinely* rational. Jesus asked Jairus to trust that a higher level of reality existed that he could not see but that was nonetheless real. And at that higher level of reality, the resurrection of a dead girl falls well within the realm of the normal, the natural, and the rational.

Faith is intelligence graduated. It is rational thinking at its most sophisticated level. Faith is not a sign of intellectual weakness but rather a sign of intellectual maturity. Higher-level reasoning always points toward faith.

Faith—What It Is and Isn't

We don't have to guess at a scriptural definition of faith. The biblical writer of Hebrews, being guided by the Holy Spirit, gave us a beautiful statement of what faith is: "Now faith is being sure of what we hope for and certain of what we do not see" (Heb. 11:1). Another translation called faith "the reality of what is hoped for, the proof of what is not seen" (HCSB). It seems that the writer of Hebrews didn't feel that faith was illogical at all. Translators have used various English words to try to communicate his high understanding of what faith is: *confidence, assurance, certainty, being sure, proof, conviction,* and *evidence.* The writer of Hebrews didn't appear to believe that faith was the result of guesswork or haphazardness. His words sound more like what a lawyer might use in a courtroom when pushing for a verdict, not the musings of a confused spiritual seeker.

Let's look at the Bible's concept of faith and see why it's not the foolhardy venture it's been labeled as.

Faith Is Not a Blind Leap in the Dark

Years ago I was hiking with my son down the treacherous backside of a mountain. We had completed a thrilling slide down a long, gentle glacier and were negotiating the lower, more dangerous portion of the mountain's descent. Loose rock, melting snow, low-lying ground cover, and sudden drop-offs marked the terrain. Missteps weren't only possible, they were likely.

I was guiding my son through one particularly difficult area. The significant amount of bushy ground cover made it difficult to see where we were going. I was moving along, slowly but cautiously, when the ground suddenly ended beneath me. I literally walked off a ledge into thin air. Amazingly, I was able to grab a branch of a bush on the face of the ledge and stop my fall. Otherwise I would have dropped thirty feet to the rocks below.

That's how many skeptics view faith. They think it leads you along, making you feel secure, and then, suddenly, whatever you had foolishly believed in disappears beneath you. Skeptics think faith is foolish because it has no merit—it's like walking off a mountain ledge.

But it's not. Faith isn't like walking off a ledge, and it's not an irresponsible leap into darkness. In fact, faith is more like hiking in the clouds. On many occasions, the mountain summit I have been climbing toward has been shrouded in clouds above me. But never—not once—have I thought the summit wasn't there. The fact that I couldn't see it didn't change the reality of its existence. I knew the mountain was there—a map, a compass, other hikers' experiences, and the trail leading up into the clouds all confirmed that for me. I'm not being irresponsible when I push on through the haze. Reason—my experience and my knowledge—tells me that the trail will lead me to the top. But in the fog, it still takes faith to keep going.

Faith Is Not Hoping Really Hard or Wishful Thinking

Some skeptics think that faith is nothing more than prolonged and misplaced hope. It's like wishful thinking on steroids. I have no doubt that such unfounded hoping goes on every day—like the guy who plays the lottery twice a week, "knowing" that this is going to be his lucky day; or me believing each year that my fighting Baylor Bears will actually beat Texas in football. That's not what faith is. Faith looks at

God's track record and deems it reasonable to bet on him yet again. It considers the promises in God's Word—hundreds of them—and determines them to still be trustworthy and reliable. Faith isn't random or meaningless hope. It's never betting on blind luck.

On December 21, 1988, when Pan Am Flight 103 was blown out of the sky by a terrorist's bomb over Lockerbie, Scotland, 259 innocent men, women, and children on the plane and 11 more on the ground lost their lives. In those terrible, agonizing moments before the plane finally crashed to earth, passengers who survived the initial explosion had to ride out the horrible fall, knowing that their death was only moments away. In those final minutes of their lives, those passengers came face-to-face with what they believed, or didn't, and with the reality of their faith, or their lack of it. This tragic truth was made painfully clear when recovery workers found many of the dead passengers still strapped into their seats—with their fingers crossed.[1]

Faith is more than just crossing your fingers. It's more than a lucky roll of the dice. Faith isn't hoping for the best or pulling on the long end of a wishbone. Faith rests in the unchanging and proven character of God.

Faith Is a Response to the Promptings of God

When Jairus led Jesus to his house, even after learning his daughter had died, he wasn't doing so of his own accord. He wasn't trying to convince Jesus to do something he couldn't or didn't want to. When Jairus took Jesus to his daughter's body, he did so because Jesus asked him to.

Faith is always a response to what God has called or commanded you to do. Moses stepped into the waters of the Red Sea because God told him to cross it. Peter stepped out of the safety of the boat onto the whitecapped waters of the Sea of Galilee because Jesus called him to. The disciples told a crowd of perhaps ten to twelve thousand men, women, and children to sit down and prepare for a meal because Jesus had just commanded them to feed those people.

The message of Christ isn't just something you choose, it's something you obey. This is a critical point about faith that skeptics don't recognize. When a seeking person embraces the claims of Christ and becomes a follower, he or she is obeying the command of God to believe in his Son. When Christ-followers stop bad habits, serve neighbors, forgive enemies, or give away significant portions of their income, they do so because they're commanded to. Believers take what seem to be, in human terms, risky or even irresponsible steps because God has told them that he will come through. Faith isn't self-initiated or human-sponsored; it's God-initiated and God-sponsored. That's why it is reasonable.

Faith Is Action, Not Simply Belief

Another reason skeptics misunderstand faith is that they think it to be a passive posture. They might mistakenly imagine that people of faith stop working for food, don't take sick children to a doctor, fail to confront problems, and basically just sit still, waiting idly for some imaginary God to come through. But passivity isn't faith. In the Bible, faith requires and assumes obedience. It produces a call to action. Faith takes the potent combination of knowledge and experience and yields a step, a decision, a movement, or an initiative. Faith is Abram leaving his hometown of Ur to go to a country he knew nothing about, Moses calling forth water from a rock, and Joshua leading the Israelites into an already occupied Promised Land—each was a direct response to the command of God. Skeptics who think people of faith are just spiritual couch sitters don't fully understand faith. People of faith are vigorous, active, and able-minded. They have to be; faith requires it.

The Biggest Problem with Faith

Here's the real reason I believe many skeptics attack God and the concept of faith in him: *control*. The most threatening thing to skeptics about faith isn't the intangibility of what they're asked to believe. It's the control issue. People of faith readily admit they've placed their confidence, their hope, their future, their provision, their security, and their happiness in something other than themselves. People of faith look to a source outside themselves to meet their ultimate needs. For a skeptic, there's nothing more terrifying. The upside of disbelieving is that you have to depend only on yourself; there is no God figure to let you down or tell you what to do. The downside is that you always have to settle for the best *you* can do. Perhaps I should explain.

Did you know that many of the world's most outspoken atheists and agnostics once claimed to be people of faith and were even active in their churches? Many skeptics formerly professed to be believers. Why is that? There is no doubt that many had their faith ambushed by the persuasive and intellectually stimulating arguments of Darwinism and materialism.[2] But beyond that, many current skeptics were burned by the church. You've heard the stories: a preacher ran off with the church secretary; a pastor sexually abused his kids; a church split over the color of the carpet; a sinner was thrown out of the church by hypocritical members. Take such major disappointments in the church—and, by extension, God—and add them to the safe and extremely predictable worldview of humanism, and you've got the perfect formula for rejecting faith.

I want to be very clear here in what I'm saying. So let me say it again, a bit more directly: many religious skeptics today, people who reject faith as unreasonable, aren't skeptical for merely scientific or intellectual reasons. More often than not, they're skeptical because they tried religion and the church and found them wanting. Their ventures into faith led to heartache, disappointment, embarrassment, and relational chaos. Such disappointments in God neither disprove nor discredit him. But they do prove that faith is a challenging walk that requires personal maturity, community, and discipleship—three areas in which many believers aren't well developed. As a result, those believers are perfect candidates for a faith crisis.

Maybe someone they loved died, and they blamed God. Maybe a "Christian" hurt them terribly. Regardless, the minds of such people reason that if that's faith, they want nothing to do with it. They gave religion, God, and the whole faith thing a chance, and they got burned in the process. As a result, they've closed their souls off to any notion of the reality of something spiritual. It's a spiritual survival technique as much as anything else. Suffice it to say that their "faith" left them spiritually bankrupt, and there's no way they're going to let that happen again. Many skeptics don't reject faith because it's irrational; they reject it simply because they don't want to believe.

The tragic experiences of such believers-turned-skeptics don't undermine faith—far from it. Rather, they support the biblical notion that we all live in a sin-filled world and we desperately need grace. But the human tendency is to *blame* God rather than *bless* him, to run *from* him rather than *to* him. To seek God in the face of our human misery would be to admit our own culpability, and that, for many, is just too bitter a pill to swallow. God makes a much more appealing villain.

But this straying from faith of many of our prodigal brothers and sisters is also an indictment of the weak and impotent form of Christianity that many of us have settled for. When the church has no compelling power, grace, forgiveness, or abundant living to model for a seeking person or new believer, what's the attraction for remaining in the fold? There isn't one. The ego-stroking pride of intellectual humanism, along with the accountability-free environment of atheism, makes for a much more pleasant environment for a person than the lame and manipulative teachings of a lukewarm church.

If we want to show our skeptical counterparts in Western culture that we're not crazy for believing, then we need to start living, loving, serving, giving, sacrificing, and even dying as Jesus commanded us to. Such biblical Christianity will go a long way toward disarming the hostile skeptics in our culture.

A Foolish Faith

There's one more aspect to faith that we need to briefly consider, and it may be the most important of all. The reality of faith is never going to make sense to a person without Christ, because he or she is blind to the ways of God's kingdom. John 3:3 tells us that when we are born again, we can see God's kingdom. The reverse is also true: when we're not born again, we can't see it. As a result, a tension is always going to exist between people who know God and those who don't, because they're looking at matters of faith through a completely different set of lenses. Remember, people without Christ are spiritually blind (see 2 Cor. 4:4); we can't expect them to find reasonable that which they cannot see or perceive.

God didn't create this spiritual blindness. Keep in mind that in Genesis 1–2, Adam and Eve had full exposure and access to God, until they rebelled against him. The blindness that affects nonbelievers was caused by sin, not God. He's the solution, not the source of the problem.

In 1 Corinthians 1–2, the apostle Paul talked at length about the tension that exists between people of the world and those who follow Christ. I suggest you read and meditate upon Paul's teachings in these two chapters, beginning with verse 18 of chapter 1. For our purposes here, let's draw some general conclusions from Paul's teachings about God's wisdom versus human wisdom.

- Human wisdom alone can never discover God. "In the wisdom of God the world through its wisdom did not know him" (1 Cor. 1:21). The wisdom of humanity will always lead away from God, not toward him. That's why millions of people think it reasonable that all life could be the result of a random series of accidents. Human wisdom will always miss the mark when it comes to discovering ultimate reality. Unbelievers simply can't discover the reality of God on their own. They need the leadership of the Holy Spirit, just as you and I as believers do.

- The wisdom of God is hidden. "We do, however, speak a message of wisdom among the mature, but not the wisdom of this age or of the rulers of this age, who are coming to nothing. No, we speak of God's secret wisdom, a wisdom that has been hidden and that God destined for our glory before time began" (1 Cor. 2:6–7). Because God is infinite and holy, he has to allow himself to be discovered; he has to lead us to him. If it were possible for us to merely think our way to God, we wouldn't need the revelation of God's mystery that we discussed in earlier chapters. As it is, the realities of God will elude us until we seek him on his terms, not ours.

- The ways of God appear foolish to an unbelieving mind. "The man without the Spirit does not accept the things that come from the Spirit of God, for they are foolishness to him, and he cannot understand them, because they are spiritually discerned" (1 Cor. 2:14). This verse sums up the tension between believers and unbelievers. Skeptics don't just not believe; they frequently attack and condemn those who do. To an unregenerate mind, faith isn't just unlikely, it's irresponsible. It's dodging reality. No wonder irreligious people criticize believers—we claim to live in and relate to a world they don't see or believe in. They're blind to it. Until they humbly respond to the revelation of the reality of God, we might as well be talking about worshiping Peter Pan or Santa Claus.

Why Faith Makes Sense

As long as you live in an unbelieving world, people are going to think that your faith is foolish. It's not. You're not crazy for believing, and don't let the onslaught of conventional wisdom tell you otherwise. If anything, the cultural resistance to your beliefs is a sign that you're on the right track. If your faith ever starts to make sense to a God-rejecting culture, you can be sure that you've set aside everything divine about your beliefs. Don't compromise your faith. Be content to live with some cultural tension, and let God deal with those in your world who reject your faith. And remember, because you believe, you're actually thinking and reasoning on a higher level than your unbelieving counterparts.

Faith isn't irrational; it's not irresponsible. Faith is actually the principles of reason—knowledge and experience—taken to their appropriate next levels. When Jesus told Jairus not to lose hope, he was calling him to think and reason on a higher plain. He was telling him that a power existed that he had yet to see but still had good reason to believe in.

So what happened to Jairus's daughter? Was his faith in vain? Had Jesus misled him? Was it irrational for Jairus to believe that his dead daughter could live again? Luke's beautiful narrative tells us the answer:

> When he [Jesus] arrived at the house of Jairus, he did not let anyone go in with him except Peter, John and James, and the child's father and mother. Meanwhile, all the people were wailing and mourning for her. "Stop wailing," Jesus said. "She is not dead but asleep." They laughed at him, knowing that she was dead. But he took her by the hand and said, "My child, get up!" Her spirit returned, and at once she stood up.
>
> Luke 8:51–55

Conclusion

Faith Makes Sense

Congratulations! You've made it to the end of this book. In the last ten chapters, we've learned that faith in God is inseparably linked to significant intellectual processes in your brain. We've seen that we are required to think and reason if we are to know God. We've learned that when God decides to make contact with a human, he typically begins with that person's mind.

We've also learned that every human is exposed each day to the reality of God. The revelation of God through nature makes the case for God undeniable and irrefutable. Beyond that, Jesus came and showed the world what God is really like. He set the record straight about God and showed us his heart. When Jesus died, he not only became the way to God for all who would believe, but he also liberated our minds from the tyranny of sin. Rather than being dimwits and numskulls, Christians actually have the capacity to think on higher, more profound levels than their unbelieving counterparts. Faith in God exposes our minds to God's heart and mind. While we'll never fully tap into his reservoir or fully comprehend him, his Holy Spirit equips us to think, dream, reason, imagine, and meditate on levels unavailable to us when we didn't yet believe. Rather than slowing down your mental synapses, belief actually enhances them.

In short, you're not crazy for your belief. Don't ever let anyone tell you that you are. I hope that after reading this book, you know and believe just how intellectually sound your faith really is.

Before we conclude, there is one final area we need to touch on. It is what's ultimately behind our culture's intellectual snobbery and disbelieving artificial intelligence. It's pride.

Are You Out of Your Mind?

How many times have you used the phrase, "They're out of their mind"? I know I've used it more times than I can count. I've used it to describe young brides making questionable marriage choices. I've used it in reference to drivers on our local roadways. I've also used it many times after watching extreme sports on ESPN. When you accuse people of being out of their mind, what are you saying? You're saying that they're not thinking. Don't you sometimes just want to grab people and yell, "THINK!"? It's like they just put their brains in neutral and set aside all reason and logic.

The Bible offers many great examples of men and women who, unfortunately, were out of their minds. One of the best is the story of King Nebuchadnezzar. Nebuchadnezzar ruled the mighty Babylonian Empire in the years preceding and during the capture and occupation of Judah.[1] Nebuchadnezzar was an unlikely tool of God, and he knew it (see Dan.

2:36–37; 4:19–27). It wasn't like his nation was known for its love and random acts of kindness. Had God been so inclined, he certainly would have had good reason to bring judgment on the Babylonians. But God had bigger fish to fry, so to speak, and he decided to use the Babylonians as an expression of judgment against the nation of Judah. And judge he did—by completely destroying Jerusalem and by deporting most of its citizens to Babylon.

The prophets made it very clear that this was an act against Judah and in no way an endorsement of Babylon's paganism or lack of morality. Nebuchadnezzar was told in no uncertain terms that he was being used as a tool of God, and if he would humble himself, God would bless his nation. But humility wasn't on Nebuchadnezzar's radar screen; the allure of power and wealth had gone to his head. One night while gazing at the massive city of Babylon and reflecting on its beauty, he said, "Is not this the great Babylon I have built as the royal residence, by my mighty power and for the glory of my majesty?" (Dan. 4:30). Bad move.

The words were still on his lips when a voice came from heaven, "This is what is decreed for you, King Nebuchadnezzar: Your royal authority has been taken from you. You will be driven away from people and will live with the wild animals; you will eat grass like cattle. Seven times will pass by for you until you acknowledge that the Most High is sovereign over the kingdoms of men and gives them to anyone he wishes."

Immediately what had been said about Nebuchadnezzar was fulfilled. He was driven away from people and ate grass like cattle. His body was drenched with the dew of heaven until his hair grew like the feathers of an eagle and his nails like the claws of a bird.

verses 31–33

For seven long years Nebuchadnezzar lived in this demented state. He was literally out of his mind. He lived and acted as if he were a wild beast. He had no awareness of his friends or family, no sense of need to fulfill his obligations as king, and no thought of acting human. Today he surely would have been institutionalized. But after the seventh year, something happened: Nebuchadnezzar came to his senses.

> At the end of that time, I, Nebuchadnezzar, raised my eyes toward heaven, and my sanity was restored. Then I praised the Most High; I honored and glorified him who lives forever. . . . At the same time that my sanity was restored, my honor and splendor were returned to me for the glory of my kingdom. My advisers and nobles sought me out, and I was restored to my throne and became even greater than before.
>
> verses 34, 36

Nebuchadnezzar admitted that when he finally turned his heart toward heaven and acknowledged the sovereignty and majesty of God, his senses were restored. He said that he regained his reason, quite literally. Looking back, the king concluded, "Now I, Nebuchadnezzar, praise and exalt and glorify the King of heaven, because everything he does is right and all his ways are just. And those who walk in pride he is able to humble" (v. 37).

Isn't that interesting? Nebuchadnezzar associated his mental downfall with his own pride and arrogance. When he didn't give due glory to God, he eventually lost his reasoning abilities. His own high opinion of himself drove him crazy. But when Nebuchadnezzar humbled himself, when he placed himself in the proper posture before God, not only did his reasoning return, but his kingdom was restored to him as well. Once again we find a biblical connection between humility before God and mental sharpness.

Pride Goes before a Fall

Sadly, much of the opposition to Christianity these days isn't based on fact or reason, it's based on pride. Ever since Genesis 3, the human ego has had relentless ambition. In the face of great learning and progress, humans have proven more likely to swell up with pride rather than bow down with humility. And it is pride, quite tragically, that leads not only to the casting off of God but also to cultural downfall.

There is no shortage of verses in the Bible that address the sin of pride and its dangers. Taking glory due to God and ascribing it to humans is setting up ourselves, our churches, our businesses, our nation—whatever we might be exalting— for major failure. Consider some of these sobering words:

> In his pride the wicked does not seek him; in all his thoughts there is no room for God.
>
> Psalm 10:4

> When pride comes, then comes disgrace, but with humility comes wisdom.
>
> Proverbs 11:2

> The LORD detests all the proud of heart. Be sure of this: They will not go unpunished.
>
> Proverbs 16:5

> The proud and arrogant man—"Mocker" is his name; he behaves with overweening pride.
>
> Proverbs 21:24

The eyes of the arrogant man will be humbled and the pride of men brought low; the Lord alone will be exalted in that day.

Isaiah 2:11

Who is it you have insulted and blasphemed? Against whom have you raised your voice and lifted your eyes in pride? Against the Holy One of Israel!

Isaiah 37:23

Son of man, say to the ruler of Tyre, "This is what the Sovereign Lord says: 'In the pride of your heart you say, "I am a god; I sit on the throne of a god in the heart of the seas." But you are a man and not a god, though you think you are as wise as a god.'"

Ezekiel 28:2

On the appointed day Herod, wearing his royal robes, sat on his throne and delivered a public address to the people. They shouted, "This is the voice of a god, not of a man." Immediately, because Herod did not give praise to God, an angel of the Lord struck him down, and he was eaten by worms and died.

Acts 12:21–23

That last verse about the worms really gets me. I try to remember it whenever I start thinking that I'm a big deal.

How Shall We Then Live?

Pride is the archenemy of many well-learned seekers. Many in the scientific and academic communities fall prey to the notion that their wisdom and learning are their own doing, the work of their own hands. Sadly, many who study our world and how humans function in it frequently become more enamored with the object of their studies than with the source of it—God. Paul noted, "They exchanged the truth of God for a lie, and worshiped and served created things rather than the Creator—who is forever praised. Amen" (Rom. 1:25).

How should we respond to such exalted thinking? How do we react to a culture that is so naturally prone to elevate man and devalue God? Let me give you a few suggestions.

First, *live humbly.* You can begin to combat the arrogance of the world by dealing with your own. If you're a believer, you're certainly not exempt from the temptation to think more of yourself than you should. When you do, you're never far from the types of infighting, church splits, and moral failures that give skeptics even more reason not to believe. If you want to push back against culture's exaltation of the human mind, then respond as Jesus did. When man rebelled against God and tried to exalt himself over God, Jesus responded by humbling himself, serving, and ultimately dying. Godly churches filled with humble, serving people will help spiritual skeptics begin to regain confidence in the message and reality of God.

Second, *share truth.* You don't have to be an expert in theology or science to communicate effectively with spiritual skeptics. The most powerful weapon you have is God's Word. Jesus promised that his truth sets people free (see John 8:32). People who oppose Christianity don't need to be wowed by new science or swayed by great philosophical arguments. They need to be convicted by God's Word. So when you talk with them about your spiritual differences, don't be shy about quoting the Bible. Let them know you believe God's Word. Share it readily with them. It is still true, even if they don't believe it. God will use his Word to convict their spirits and woo them to himself.

If you're going to share scriptural truth with spiritual skeptics, then you have to be familiar with the Scriptures. Read the Bible—study it, meditate on it, read books about it. Many Christ-followers feel intimidated by those who oppose Christianity because they themselves are biblically illiterate. They have neither the biblical knowledge nor the faith that comes with it to stand their ground. If you want to have a strong and robust faith in the face of cultural opposition, and if you want to communicate effectively with the spiritual skeptics in your world, then get to know God's Word. Learn to *think* biblically.

Finally, *pray*. Those who doubt the validity of the gospel need prayer; those who defend it need it as well. Pray that the skeptics in your world will have their eyes opened by the power of Christ. Ask God to free them from their mental blindness that Satan has caused. Pray that he would humble them. Pray also for yourself and other believers as you try to articulate your faith. Pray that your confidence won't waver in the face of the ongoing media onslaught that questions the veracity of your faith.

A Word to Skeptics and Seekers

If you're not a Christ-follower, thank you for reading this book. I want to assure you that you're not foolish for considering the reality of God. The world you live in, the air you breathe, and the brain you're using right now to process these letters and words are not the results of some giant cosmic accident. There is more to life than what you can see, and every day that you consider the plausibility of God moves you one step closer to discovering his reality.

God loves you more than you can ever fully know or understand. That's the heart of the Bible's message: "For God so loved the world that he gave his one and only Son, that whoever believes in him shall not perish but have eternal life" (John 3:16). God created you and loves you as you are right now. He desires to have a relationship with you.

Finally, I'd like you to try something. I'd like you to try talking to God, even if you're not sure he exists. You're not going to insult him or make him mad because you're still not sure you believe. Remember that you're not the first doubter to try to find him. God will honor your attempt to reach out to him. You have faith, even if it seems small, and I'm asking you to approach God on the basis of that. He'll do the rest.

Try this: find a quiet and private place and get alone, maybe in your bedroom, maybe under a tree somewhere, maybe under a brilliant night sky. Stand, sit, or kneel; it doesn't matter. Turn your hands palms up, toward heaven. That's a sign of submission, humility, and even dependence, and it's the perfect posture to assume when approaching God. Then talk to God out loud. He can hear your thoughts, but it will be easier for you to focus if you talk out loud. Tell him about your struggles with faith. Tell him you're having trouble believing. Then say something like this: "God, if you're real, please show me. If the evidence is there and I'm just missing it, then please open my eyes so I can see you. God, if you truly exist, then I don't want to live life without you. So please make yourself real to me. Show me your power and glory, and please show me the reality of your Son, Jesus. I want to know you, God. Help me to believe."

I don't know what will happen when you pray that prayer. The wind may blow harder; you may get goose bumps; the hair on the back of your neck may stand up; you may feel very peaceful. Or nothing may happen. You may not feel a thing. But God will answer your prayer. He will make himself real to you. It might be a day, a week, a month, or a year later, but he will answer you. God will step into your world in a way that is clear and undeniable.

So go ahead and pray. Ask God to introduce himself to you. You have nothing to lose and everything to gain.

Why Faith Makes Sense

Time is on the side of truth, and truth is on the side of God. Your faith is valid because what it's based on is true. I have no doubt that eternity, if not time, will prove the claims of Christ to be legitimate. Meanwhile, keep standing firm in your faith. And the next time someone tells you they don't believe in God, ask *them* to explain why. Then make sure you have plenty of time, because you're going to be in for a long conversation. Yea, God.

Notes

Introduction

1. Sam Harris, *Letter to a Christian Nation* (New York: Alfred A. Knopf, 2006), xii.

2. Richard Dawkins, *The God Delusion* (New York: Houghton Mifflin, 2006), 100.

Chapter 1 Everyone Loves a Good Mystery

1. *Webster's New Collegiate Dictionary*, s.v. "Mystery."

2. Ibid.

3. *Merriam Webster Dictionary Online*, s.v. "Mystery," http://www.m-w.com/dictionary/mystery.

4. For examples of Paul's use of *mystery*, see Ephesians 1:9; 3:3–4, 6, 9; 6:19; and Colossians 1:26.

Chapter 2 Contact

1. When I say *revelation*, I'm not referring to the famous last book of the Bible. The book of Revelation is a record of what John the disciple saw in a series of visions while in exile on the Greek isle of Patmos. God *revealed* to John what would happen on the earth and to all its inhabitants during what is known as the "end times." The last book of the Bible is called *Revelation* because it contains information that John couldn't

have gotten any other way. Had God not shown John what was going to occur, then he—and by extension, we—would never know.

2. Sharon Begley, "Your Brain on Religion: Mystic Visions or Brain Circuits at Work?" *Newsweek*, May 7, 2001, http://www.cognitiveliberty .org/neuro/neuronewswk.htm.

Chapter 3 Rocky Mountain High

1. Michael Behe, *Darwin's Black Box* (New York: Free Press, 1996), 232.

2. E. W. F. Tomlin, quoted in Ronald Duncan and Miranda Weston Smith, eds., *The Encyclopedia of Ignorance* (New York: Pergamon, 1977), 227.

3. James Tour, quoted in Lee Strobel, *The Case for Faith* (Grand Rapids: Zondervan, 2000), 111.

4. Alan Hayward, *Creation and Evolution* (Minneapolis: Bethany House, 1985), 65, emphasis his.

5. Fred Heeren, *Show Me God* (Wheeling, IL: Searchlight Publications, 1995), 61.

6. Robert Jastrow, *God and the Astronomers*, 2nd ed. (New York: W. W. Norton, 1992), 105.

7. See Romans 1:18–20.

8. The Barna Group, "Beliefs: General Religious," 2007, http://www .barna.org/FlexPage.aspx?Page=Topic&TopicID=2.

Chapter 4 Tracks in the Snow

1. Blaise Pascal, *Pensées*, part 3, http://en.wikipedia.org/wiki/ Pascal's_Wager#_note-0.

Chapter 5 How Did We Get Here?

1. Dave Panos, personal written testimony, Austin Christian Fellowship, March 2002. Used by permission.

2. Richard Dawkins, "The Illusion of Design," *Natural History*, November 2005, http://www.naturalhistorymag.com/master.html?http:// www.naturalhistorymag.com/1105/1105_feature1.html.

3. "A Scientific Dissent from Darwinism," Center for Science and Culture, www.dissentfromdarwin.org.

4. *The Week*, September 8, 2006, 18.

5. Sam Harris, "Letter to a Christian Nation," www.randomhouse
.com/kvpa/harris/ltcn_quotes.php.

6. For great reading from the more scientific side of this debate, see
Lee Strobel, *The Case for a Creator* (Grand Rapids: Zondervan, 2005)
and *The Case for Faith* (Grand Rapids: Zondervan, 2000); Fred Heeren,
Show Me God (Wheeling, IL: Searchlight Publications, 1995); Phillip
Johnson, *Darwin on Trial* (Downers Grove, IL: InterVarsity Press, 1993);
Jobe Martin, *The Evolution of a Creationist* (Rockwall, TX: Biblical Dis-
cipleship Publishers, 2004); Francis Collins, *The Language of God* (New
York: Free Press, 2006); Michael Behe, *Darwin's Black Box* (New York:
Free Press, 1996); Thomas Woodward, *Doubts about Darwin* (Grand
Rapids: Baker, 2003); and Werner Gitt, *Did God Use Evolution?* (Green
Forest, AR: New Leaf Publishing, 2006).

7. The phrase "according to their kinds [or 'its kind']" appears nine
times in the first chapter of Genesis (see vv. 11, 12, 21, 24, and 25). For
instance, Genesis 1:21 says, "So God created the great creatures of the sea
and every living and moving thing with which the water teems, according
to their kinds, and every winged bird according to its kind. And God saw
that it was good." Notice that the phrase is used after the creation of sea
creatures and birds. The implication of this phrase in all these verses is
that God set boundaries—specifically, genetic boundaries—around the
species of birds, fish, plants, and, of course, humans.

The Bible seems to allow for change and variation within a certain
species, but it does not allow for variation between species. In other
words, cats may change and evolve, but they will always be cats. Cats
cannot and will not become something else—say, a bird or a dog. The
repeated phrase "according to their kinds [or 'its kind']" makes a strong
biblical case for micro-, but not macro-, evolution.

8. Strobel, *The Case for Faith*, 47.

9. Johnson, *Darwin on Trial*, 45.

10. Ibid., 46.

11. Ibid., 50.

Chapter 6 Who's in Charge Here?

1. Christopher Phillips, quoted in Anita Hamilton, "All the Right Questions," *Time*, April 5, 2004, 65–66.

2. In this chapter, I offer an overview of humanism and the differences between human-centered and God-centered worldviews. This
is in no way intended to be a comprehensive discussion of humanism.

While key points in the discussion have obviously been left out (a full discussion could easily fill the book), enough critical content has been included to give the reader a good understanding of the major thrust and emphases of humanism.

3. "The Affirmations of Humanism: A Statement of Principles," Council for Secular Humanism, 2008, http://www.secularhumanism.org/index.php?section=main&page=affirmations.

4. Council for Secular Humanism, homepage, 2008, http://www.secularhumanism.org/index.php.

5. "A Secular Humanist Declaration," Council for Secular Humanism, 2008, http://www.secularhumanism.org/index.php?section=main&page=declaration.

6. Ibid.

7. Jeffery Kluger, "What Makes Us Moral," *Time*, December 3, 2007, 54.

8. Michael D. Lemonick and Andrea Dorfman, "Up from the Apes: Remarkable New Evidence Is Filling In the Story of How We Became Human," *Time*, August 23, 1999, http://www.time.com/time/magazine/article/0,9171,991790,00.html.

Chapter 7 A Thinking Person's Guide to Faith

1. It is not my purpose here to offer a comprehensive defense of the Bible itself as the sourcebook for the Christian faith. Many great works written by minds far superior to mine already exist. If you're interested in reading up on the historical credibility of the Bible, you might consider reading the following: Greg Boyd, *Letters from a Skeptic* (Colorado Springs: Cook Communications, 1994); Cliff Knechtle, *Give Me an Answer That Satisfies My Heart and My Mind* (Downers Grove, IL: InterVarsity Press, 1986); Chad Meister, *Building Belief* (Grand Rapids: Baker, 2006); F. F. Bruce, *The Canon of Scripture* (Downers Grove, IL: InterVarsity Press, 1988), and *Answers to Questions* (Grand Rapids: Zondervan, 1972). Or you can visit http://www.everystudent.com/features/bible.html and http://www.carm.org/bible.htm.

2. The term *canon* means "standard," "rule," or "law." Books became part of the authoritative standard, or canon, of the church only after they gained wide acceptance by early church leaders and councils.

3. For a thorough discussion of the historical and documentary support for the New Testament, see F. F. Bruce, *The New Testament Documents: Are They Reliable?* (Grand Rapids: Eerdmans, 2003).

4. C. S. Lewis, quoted in Wayne Martindale and Jerry Root, eds., *The Quotable C. S. Lewis* (Wheaton: Tyndale, 1989), 124.

5. Ibid., 125.

6. C. S. Lewis, *Mere Christianity* (New York: MacMillan, 1952), 52–53.

Chapter 8 God's Self-Portrait

1. See also John 1:14; 5:17–18; 8:58; 14:8–9; 20:26–29; Colossians 1:15–18; 2:9; Philippians 2:5–11; and Hebrews 1:1–3.

Chapter 9 Name Above All Names

1. The Jesus Seminar is a self-named group of scholars who seriously doubt the biblical records of Jesus. For a fair evaluation and further information on the Jesus Seminar, go to http://www.leaderu.com/of fices/billcraig/docs/rediscover1.html; http://www.jesus.com.au/library/ jesus_seminar/gospels.php; and http://www.ovrlnd.com/FalseTeaching/ jesusseminar.html.

2. Thomson Reuters, "Kathy Griffin's Jesus Remark Cut from Emmy Show," September 11, 2007, http://www.reuters.com/article/television News/idUSN1144512920070911.

3. David W. Boles, "Jesus Found Dead in His Grave," David W. Boles's Urban Semiotic, February 25, 2007, http://urbansemiotic.com/ 2007/02/25/jesus-found-dead-in-his-grave/.

4. For a thorough discussion of the historical case for the resurrection, see Greg Boyd, *Letters from a Skeptic* (Colorado Springs: Cook Communications, 1994), and Lee Strobel, *The Case for Christ* (Grand Rapids: Zondervan, 1998).

Chapter 10 A Beautiful Mind

1. Rod Nordland, "The Last Victims," *Newsweek*, February 12, 2001, 21.

2. Materialism is the belief that only the material/physical world is real. There is no spiritual/eternal world in a materialistic mind-set.

Conclusion

1. Judah was the southern kingdom after Israel and Judah split into two kingdoms in 922 BC. Israel, the northern kingdom, fell to the Assyrians in 722 BC. Judah fell to Nebuchadnezzar and the Babylonians in 586 BC.

Will Davis Jr. is the founding and senior pastor of Austin Christian Fellowship in Austin, Texas. Will and his wife, Susie, have three children.

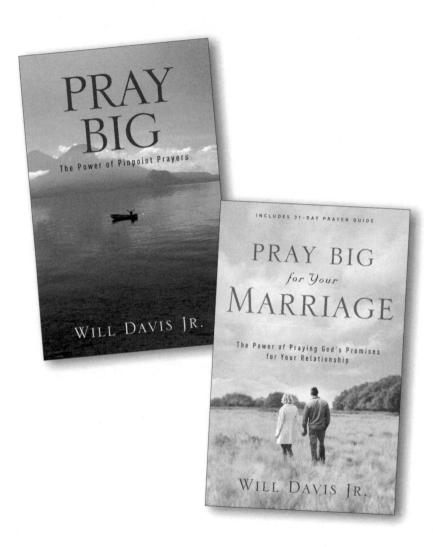